Seafood Lover's Bible

Seafood Lover's Bible

Michael F. Bavota

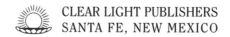

CLEAR LIGHT PUBLISHERS
SANTA FE, NEW MEXICO

Clear Light Publishers, 823 Don Diego, Santa Fe, NM 87501
WEB: www.clearlightbooks.com

First Edition
10 9 8 7 6 5 4 3 2 1

Library of Congress Cataloging-in-Publication Data

Bavota, Michael F., 1952-
    Seafood lover's bible / Michael F. Bavota.
        p. cm.
    ISBN 1-57416-027-3
    1. Cookery (Seafood)   2. Seafood   I. Title.
TX747.B346   1999
641.6'92—dc21   99-18051
                                                                      CIP

Drawings:

Rhode Island Seafood Council (Wendy Andrews), pages 5, 10, 17, 19, 47, 55, 57, 58, 59, 69, 80, 92, 97, 101, 108, 118, 121, 132, 144, 175

Alaska Seafood Marketing Institute, pages 3, 40, 78

Florida Department of Agriculture and Consumer Services, pages 26, 39, 40, 48, 59, 63, 84, 87, 89, 107, 116, 130, 149

Our Living Oceans (U.S. Department of Commerce, 1993), pages 72, 73

Cover photo © Jeff Burak, Stock Market Photo Agency
Cover design: Carol O'Shea
Typography and Design: Mary Rose and Carol O'Shea

Printed in Canada

DEDICATION AND ACKNOWLEDGMENTS

This book is dedicated to my great friend Phil Melfi, a businessman of high integrity, who has given me unwavering and uncompromising support throughout my career.

Special thanks go to those who helped with the fish facts that are so valuable to this cookbook: Karla Ruzicka, Chief, U.S. Department of Commerce/NOAA; Joanne McNeely, Bureau Chief, Florida Bureau of Seafood and Aquaculture; Gary Bower and Mark Jones, The Alaskan Seafood Marketing Institute; and Ralph Boragine, Executive Director, Rhode Island Seafood Council.

Special thanks are also due my publisher, Harmon Houghton, who supported the idea of this book from day one and created the excitement within his staff during its evolution. I wish to thank my wonderful editor, Sara Held, who provided a careful blending of cookbook expertise and a gentle yet confident touch to guide the shaping of this book. It is a pleasure to work with everyone at Clear Light Publishers.

CONTENTS

Chapter II CRAB 38

Chapter III LOBSTER 47

Chapter IV OTHER SHELLFISH 53

ABOUT THIS BOOK

READ THIS BEFORE YOU COOK

Throughout the past decade, a number of foods deemed "good" for your health have made news headlines. These foods quickly become the newest fad for better health, and are consumed by many in the quest to live longer and feel better. Yet, after a closer look with more conclusive evidence, these highly touted foods often turn out to be less beneficial than we thought. Some are even found later to be unsafe. So what is safe to eat? What is good to eat? One food that has been around since water appeared on the face of the earth and has been proven time and again to be good for your heart is *seafood*.

On October 31, 1995, the *Journal of the American Medical Association* reported, "One serving of fatty-fish per week can reduce the risk of cardiac arrest by 50–70 percent." In May 1995, the *Journal* also released the results of an extensive, twenty-year study of the relationship between seafood consumption and coronary heart disease. The study shows that among Greenland Eskimos, who regularly eat about 400 grams of seafood per day, there were low rates of death from coronary heart disease.

At a recent American Heart Association convention, University of Washington research professor Santica Marcovina presented strong evidence that a diet heavy in fish can reduce blood pressure, cholesterol, and heart-threatening fat even better than vegetarian diets (from *Seafood Source*, National Fisheries Institute, Winter 1998). The fish that contribute the most to good health are discussed below in **Healthy Choices**.

Even with strong scientific evidence that seafood is a food that promotes health, yearly per capita consumption in the United States has stagnated during the past ten years at 14.8 pounds edible weight. In contrast, the Japanese consume 147.7 pounds per capita each year. American consumers eat more melons (17.0 pounds) and ice cream (15.7 pounds) than fish, a 1994 government statistic reveals. (See **Basic Seafood Knowledge**, below.)

When American consumers are asked why they eat less seafood than foods from other groups, the most common reply by far is fear of spoiling it during cooking. The truth is that seafood is expensive, and if it is not cooked successfully in the home, the household food dollar can be sacrificed for a less than enjoyable meal. In this cookbook, you will learn how to prepare good seafood in the home, easily and with great success.

The 200 seafood recipes in this book have been specifically designed to be simple enough for any average cook in the household, from mom, to bachelor, to inspired teen chef. Requiring minimal investment in cooking gear and using ingredients that can be found in most neighborhood supermarkets, the recipes are designed to satisfy your family and guests and to look great on your dinner table. Each meal is quick, full of wonderful flavor, and practically foolproof.

One of the best-kept secrets about cooking seafood is that most consumers tend to overcook the product. Purely out of habit, most home cooks treat seafood as if it were beef, chicken, or pork. We have often been warned that meat must be cooked well done if we are to avoid getting sick. Fish needs to be cooked to doneness, but the fact is: fish takes a shorter time to cook because it contains more water than meat does. The key to preparing seafood successfully in your home is to cook it just as long as needed and no longer. A simple rule for all methods of cooking seafood is the Canadian Cooking Rule: 10 minutes per inch of thickness. (See **Guide to Buying, Handling, and Cooking Seafood,** below.)

The first eleven chapters of this book are broken down into easy species categories, beginning with everyone's favorites—shrimp, crab, and lobster—and continuing with other shellfish and individual types of fish found in the average supermarket and especially sought for home cooking. In each main species category, the first recipe provided is the easiest to prepare and offers a basic, easy method of preparation that helps give you a good feel for proper timing in cooking. At the beginning of each new category you will find background information on the seafood you will be preparing.

Other chapters are devoted to fish that are popular in different regions; now and then they may turn up in your supermarket and are worth exploring. Recipes for various types of fish soups and salads are also offered, as well as interesting seafood combinations, party dishes, and holiday specialties. To ensure a good result, the recipes include tips on how to judge when the cooking is going right and when there may be a problem. Methods of cleaning and preparing seafood for cooking are included. The recipes are designed to teach you how to work with each type of seafood successfully. Once you have mastered them, you can produce your own delicious variations—and you may become the best seafood cook in your neighborhood. My hope is that you will try these recipes and learn how very easy it is to prepare seafood successfully in the home. And do your heart a favor: EAT MORE SEAFOOD.

BASIC SEAFOOD FACTS

SEAFOOD CLASSIFICATIONS

Seafood is grouped into two basic classifications: *finfish* and *shellfish*. Finfish includes all species we normally describe as "fish"—such as salmon, tuna, cod, flounder, sea bass, and trout. Shellfish are broken down into two types: *crustaceans* and *mollusks*. Crustaceans are animals that have external skeletons with jointed legs and typically capture food with their claws and mouth. Seafood crustaceans include various species of the ever-popular shrimp, lobster, and crab, as well as crawfish. Mollusks live inside hard shells. The most popular species— clams, oysters, mussels, and scallops—feed by filtering large quantities of water for plankton and other small organisms.

GLOBAL SEAFOOD RESOURCES

Less than twenty years ago, the richest fishing grounds in the world sat deep in the North Atlantic just 200 miles off the coast of New England and Newfoundland. Fishermen throughout the world know the areas as the George's Bank and the Grand Banks. The cod family group, including haddock and hake, was so abundant that this one commodity by itself provided a rich economic base for the New England states in America, the eastern provinces of Canada, and the entire country of Iceland. In recent years the virtual collapse of that enormous fishing resource has sent centuries-old fishing towns in these areas into near ruin. As shown in the table on page 5, the decline in catch reached drastic proportions between 1982 and 1984:

Fish landings, 1982 and 1994

Species	Year	Landing In Pounds
Cod	1982	116,906,000
	1994	38,653,000
Haddock	1982	42,021,600
	1994	724,000

Source: *Report on Status of U.S. Living Marine Resources 1993*, National Marine Fisheries Service (NMFS).

Haddock

Much of the depletion was due to overfishing. Modern factory trawlers canvas the ocean bottom with miles of nets and manage to capture most of what swims. During the "heyday" of North Atlantic fishing, the resource was not managed. Fishing fleets simply caught all they could haul, with little thought of the impact on the stock.

Now fishing has been shut down in some places. Industry- and government-managed efforts over the past five years may give the fish stock a chance to rebound. As a result of restrictive measures, seafood fishing vessels, shore-side fish processors, restaurants, and super-markets have had to source the fish from all over the world to satisfy the needs of their businesses. Today seafood is truly a "global resource."

Consumer demand throughout the world is still strong for North Atlantic codfish and similar fish. Fortunately, alternative species such as orange roughy, Pacific cod, and Chilean sea bass have provided consumers with choices that ten years ago were underutilized, considered to be "trash by-catch" by the fishermen. In years past, attempts to bring these less popular fish to market ended in little demand for the product. Worldwide consumption of seafood, because of its good health attributes, has increased in the past decade, however, and made alternative species more acceptable. Countries that have always consumed huge amounts of seafood continue to do so. Countries where seafood has taken a back seat to beef, chicken, and pork are demanding more fresh seafood every day.

Annual per capita consumption of fish and shellfish for human food, 1991-93 average (live weight equivalent)

Major World Powers

Country	Region	Pounds	Kilogram
Iceland	Europe	202.4	91.8
Greenland	North America	181.4	82.3
Japan	Asia	147.7	67.0
Spain	Europe	83.8	38.0
Chile	Latin America	65.7	29.8
France	Europe	63.9	29.0
Canada	North America	50.7	23.0
U.S.A.	North America	48.1	21.8
Russia (federation)	Europe	41.7	18.9
United Kingdom	Europe	40.8	18.5
Germany	Europe	27.6	12.5
*China	Asia	27.3	12.4

†Island Countries

Maldives	Asia	277.3	125.8
Tokelau	Oceania	228.6	103.7
Palau	Oceania	205.9	93.4
British Virgin Islands	Caribbean	175.3	79.5

Source: Food and Agriculture Organization of the United Nations (FAO), *Yearbook of Fishery Statistics 1994*, vol. 78, Rome.

* China: Most of the seafood China produces is exported; therefore per capita consumption is low.
† Island Countries: Ready availability of seafood in sparsely populated areas usually results in high per capita consumption.

AQUACULTURE

Considering the rapid declines in wild global fish stocks, one would expect the world fishing industry to be in ruins. This scenario is far from being realized, however. Aquaculture, the "farm-raising" of fish and shellfish, has helped to stabilize the industry, offering record production levels over the past five years.

There are three forms of aquaculture production: *extensive,* which requires the least amount of human intervention and relies more on natural environment; *semi-intensive,* which requires minimal intervention; and *intensive*, requiring full human intervention from start to finish. The growth rate of the fish is controlled using specially engineered food. As a result, farmed seafood products tend to be higher yielding in edible flesh than wild seafood, and undesirable taste characteristics found in the wild version can be scientifically improved.

By 1995, the total production of cultured finfish, shellfish, and aquatic plants had increased by nearly 10 percent from the years 1990 to 1991. Much of the reported increase comes from low-income food-deficient countries, especially China, where most of the farm-raised product is exported.

Today, aquaculture finfish and shellfish for food represent over one quarter of the total world supply of seafood. China, India, and Japan account for 63.4 percent of the total world production. Farm-raised Atlantic salmon (*Salmo salar*), catfish, Chinese white shrimp (*Penaeus chinensis*), and tiger shrimp (*Penaeus monodon*) are the most consumed of all farm-raised seafood.

Several mainstay seafood items provided by aquaculture

Species	Major Countries Producing Product
Atlantic salmon	Chile, Norway, U.S.A., Canada, Ireland, United Kingdom, Scotland
Coho salmon	U.S.A. Washington, British Columbia, Chile
Catfish	U.S.A. Mississippi Delta region
Rainbow Trout	U.S.A. Idaho, Japan, Denmark
Tilapia	Costa Rica, Columbia, SW-South U.S.A.
Oysters	U.S.A. California, Alaska, British Columbia
Mussels	U.S.A. Maine, Holland, Spain, Canada
Hybrid Striped Bass	U.S.A. Pacific coast
White Shrimp	China, Japan
Tiger Shrimp	India, Indonesia, Pakistan, Philippines, Thailand
Crawfish	South U.S.A. Louisiana, Pacific Northwest

HOW SAFE IS SEAFOOD?

In 1992 and 1995 two well-known periodical publications ran feature articles on the safety of seafood. Both articles offered the evidence they had researched, and each produced testimonies from those who told about becoming ill after consuming seafood. Many consumers wonder,

"Will I get sick from eating seafood?" The latest studies conducted by the FDA and the CDCP (Center for Disease Control and Prevention) involving these issues have attempted to provide answers. However, since food-borne illness is often associated with poor food-handling practices rather than the food itself, conclusive judgments are difficult to make. As with any high-protein food there are certain risks that could be associated with seafood. This is what some government officials have said about the safety of seafood consumption:

In a statement made in 1992, David Kessler, M.D., Commissioner of the Food and Drug Administration, said: "The perception that seafood is unsafe is untrue. In fact...the vast preponderance of seafood that reaches the consumer is safe, clean, and free of contaminants and chemicals." Dr. Kessler was looking at evidence based on the reported and confirmed incidence of food-borne illness from seafood. The majority of these cases are associated with molluscan shellfish: clams and oysters. Even more specific is that most of the severe reported cases involved persons with compromised immune systems who ate these foods raw.

Generally seafood is very safe to eat, says Phillip Spiller, director of the Food and Drug Administration's Office of Seafood. "On a pound-for-pound basis, seafood is as safe as, if not more safe than, other meat sources. But no food is completely safe, and problems do occur."

When compared to other high-protein food categories—beef, pork, chicken, lamb, and veal—the risk of food-borne illness resulting from consuming seafood (with the exception of raw oysters, clams, and mussels) is significantly lower.

What you need to know about raw shellfish

In most instances of confirmed illness, consumption of raw shellfish is involved. Yet not all shellfish is a source of concern. Only a few species in the molluscan family—oysters, clams, and mussels—require special caution. These animals are filter feeders.

A single mussel, clam, or oyster can filter up to 15 gallons of water a day to receive its food. If water contamination or a marine virus or bacteria exists in the area where these animals feed, there is a real danger of a toxin or virus being consumed by humans. However, proper cooking kills bacteria and viruses. The highest risk of becoming ill comes from eating oysters, clams, and mussels raw. Yet many consumers do enjoy their shellfish raw everyday, without incidence of illness. Consumers should weigh the risks associated with eating raw shellfish. (See the warning issued by the FDA regarding raw molluscan shellfish, below.)

In coastal states, where many people eat raw shellfish, the incidence of illness related to raw shellfish is relatively low compared to illness caused by other high-protein perishable foods. There is a simple explanation for this. All molluscan shellfish harvested in the United States fall under the state-by-state mandated National Shellfish Sanitation Program (NSSP). Each day, the state marine agency responsible for the program monitors water conditions in every state that harvests oysters, clams, or mussels. All of these animals grow in certain areas of bays, oceans, and rivers known as "beds." When water conditions are found to be unacceptable for harvest due to storm run-off, red tide (a naturally occurring marine algae bloom), or other contamination, the beds in those areas are closed. The system has a long history of successful operation.

The Food and Drug Administration issued a fact sheet (February 8, 1993), advising on the consumption of raw molluscan shellfish. The FDA states that any animal protein consumed raw carries a higher potential for causing illness than if cooked, but that most illnesses that result are not life threatening, ranging from mild intestinal disorders to acute gastroenteritis. More serious illnesses are rare in otherwise healthy individuals. The main sources of all these illnesses are bacteria and viruses that are present in water due to human pollution. The FDA warns that people whose immune systems are compromised should avoid eating raw or partially cooked molluscan shellfish. These people are susceptible to potentially life-threatening illnesses caused by naturally occurring marine bacteria from the *Vibrio* species, particularly *Vibrio vulnificus*. People unsure of their medical status should consult their physician before consuming raw or partially cooked shellfish.

Brochures on the subject of raw shellfish and related concerns can be obtained through the FDA Seafood Hotline, at 1-800-FDA-4010 (202-205-4314), or from FDA district offices throughout the United States.

Safety note on scombroid fish

Tuna, along with mackerel, mahi-mahi, and bluefish, are in the family of fish known as *Scombroidae*, which MUST BE KEPT COLD, **under 40 degrees, during harvest and processing and until cooked.** This family of fish produces the naturally occurring marine biotoxin histadine. If the temperature requirement is not met, the histadine changes to histamine. Persons with respiratory challenges can have reactions to the high histamine levels and develop difficulty in breathing. Seafood processors, retailers and restaurants are aware of these important safety concerns and therefore strive to keep all seafood at temperatures that are best for the product. When you buy scombroid fish or any other seafood in the summer months, it is best to return home promptly and refrigerate it. Otherwise, you should carry a cooler in your car and ask the seafood clerk to provide some ice in a bag for your fish. Any reputable retailer will be happy to assist you in making sure your seafood arrives home thoroughly chilled.

Hazard Analysis Critical Control Point (HACCP)

A new seafood safety program that was made mandatory for all seafood processors in the United States, and is used effectively in many other countries, is HACCP. This inspection system requires all seafood processors to design and implement a food production plan that will identify potential food hazards and inhibit them from reaching the product. The FDA estimates that more than half of the seafood eaten in the United States is imported from 135 other countries. All seafood entering the United States must now have been produced under an HACCP plan.

GUIDE TO BUYING, HANDLING, AND COOKING SEAFOOD

WHERE TO BUY YOUR SEAFOOD

Good seafood can easily be found in many areas of the marketplace today. Except in the coastal states, finding seafood in the average supermarket was nearly impossible as recently as the late seventies. Today there are approximately 30,000 supermarkets throughout the country, and nearly one-half of them sell seafood on ice at a service counter. The others offer fresh tray-pack seafood in the meat department or frozen seafood in self-service freezer units. In addition, there are hundreds of local seafood stores, perhaps one in your town.

So who has the freshest and best fish? Is it the local fish market or the local supermarket? Only an evaluation by you—once you know what to look for—will answer that question. In most cases, freshness of seafood is not so much a matter of when it was harvested, but rather a matter of condition. Both markets may start off with the same fresh seafood, for it all swims in the same place. It is how well the supplier of each market handles his product—especially how well he keeps it cold—that determines freshness when it reaches the store. Then it is up to the merchant to handle the fish carefully, keeping it well iced and selling quickly to ensure that you get seafood in the freshest condition.

The choice of where to buy is yours. Finding out which retailer in your town offers the best product to suit your needs is simply a matter of shopping around.

USE YOUR SENSES

Smell: You should not notice any offensive fishy odors when you walk into a seafood store or a supermarket. Good, fresh seafood has a neutral or salty smell of the sea at best. Offensive odors reaching your nose upon reaching the store or the seafood counter at the supermarket are a sign of old fish and poor daily sanitation practices.

Look: Someone should be there to greet you and to help you make choices. Notice the clothes that the attendant is wearing. They must be clean. The clerk needs to be wearing a hat or a hair net when handling food. The counter person should not be smoking, eating, or drinking beverages. All of these things can transport germs and bacteria to your food. The facility should be free from insects.

Assuming there are no offensive odors, study the seafood on display. The display should look bright and shiny. The products should be displayed on a clean bed of ice. If what you see is dull, discolored fish, with ragged workmanship and a dried-out appearance, perhaps this is a good reason to pass this store by and try the next. What you are looking for in choosing your fish store is a place that sells seafood in a serious way. A store committed to selling the best seafood will pass the smell test and present a bright, professional, friendly atmosphere for the shopper.

Listen: Ask the attendant any questions you have about the product. Your choice of seafood stores should have counter personnel who are knowledgeable about the products. You should feel comfortable with them and with that store. If you feel good about the seafood display and the store, then this is the place where you should shop. As you get to know the staff and they get to know you, they will help you learn as much about seafood as you want to know. Realize that their success depends on your returning to their store to buy seafood. Most good seafood clerks enjoy sharing what they know about fish, and the good ones tell the truth. If you ask if the fish is fresh today, they will give you the truth. You may hear some say, "That fish is okay, but this fish over here is fresher today." This is the kind of customer/retailer relationship that will help you get the quality of seafood that suits you best.

GOOD SEAFOOD: QUALITY AND FRESHNESS

Live fish have a protective system that controls enzymes and inhibits bacteria from attacking their flesh. Once the fish is harvested and dies, these protections cease to function. Now the natural bacteria and enzymes in the fish begin to attack the flesh and are responsible for the aging process of the fish. At this point, the freshness and quality of the seafood are matters of *time, temperature,* and *handling.* Assuming that these things are managed successfully by the store you have selected to purchase your fish, the following conditions should be found:

Fresh whole fish

Look	Smell	Touch	Good Seafood	Poor Seafood
EYES			Clear, bright, rounded, dark pupils	Sunken, dull, cloudy
SCALES			Shiny, tight	Many missing, dry
	ODOR		Salty, sweet high-tide seashore smell	Low-tide, ammonia, rancid, stale smell
GILLS			Ruby red, dark pinkish, clear mucus	Chocolate color, brownish-yellow mucus
FLESH		FLESH	Bright, smooth tissue, finger indent springs back to touch	Dull, dried, torn or gapping tissue, finger indent remains
BELLY CAVITY	BELLY CAVITY		Clean of extraneous materials, bright, smooth, white or pinkish, smells fresh	Pieces of body organs remaining, bones sticking through belly, discolored, fishy smell, putrid

Fresh fillets or steak fish

FLESH			Tight with no gapping or fissures in meat, no dark or grayish belly membrane remaining, no bruising	Torn meat, wide fissures, pieces or entire membrane on flesh, bruising
	ODOR		Salty, sweet high-tide seashore smell	Low-tide, ammonia, rancid, stale smell
COLOR			Bright, shiny, no browning or rust colors	Dull, dry looking, brown spots or rust color in places
		FLESH	Slick, oily, pliable without breaking meat	Gummy, tacky, meat splits easily when fillet is bent slightly

Note: Fillets account for approximately 20 percent of supermarket seafood sales. The majority of fillets are boneless or practically boneless.

Fresh or freshly thawed headless shrimp

Look	Smell	Touch	Good Seafood	Poor Seafood
SHELLS			Shiny, slick-wet, bright colors, unbroken sections along back	Dull, slimy, black spots;* broken sections along back; dried-out salt look
MEAT		MEAT	White to off-white; smooth, firm, slick or oily to touch	Brownish, slimy, soft, mushy, gummy to the touch
	BODY		Neutral to somewhat grassy	Rancid, ammonia

*Pink, white, and brown shrimp will appear whitish or off white to the untrained eye. Only black tiger shrimp will show black or bluish striping.

Live shellfish (clam, lobster, crab, mussel)

Look	Smell	Touch	Good Seafood	Poor Seafood
CRAB and LOBSTER		CRAB and LOBSTER	Legs and claws moving when animal is disturbed, or is swimming in a tank	Animal appears lifeless, no response when touched
CLAM and OYSTER	CLAM and OYSTER	CLAM and OYSTER	React quickly to the touch, shells snap shut; sweet smell of high tide	Shells remain open when touched; low-tide, sewer gas-like smell
MUSSEL		MUSSEL	Bright, black shiny shells; shells close slowly when touched, but do close tight*	Dry; muddy looking; whitish shells; shells stay open after being touched

*Mussels react more slowly when touched than clams. Mussels enjoy breathing air and tend to gap to do so. You may see them gapping on ice. Ask the seafood clerk to check the mussels given to you to be sure all are alive. When mussels are touched they tend to close slowly, but finally do shut tight.

FRESH VERSUS FROZEN SEAFOOD

Frozen seafood, if properly prepared at sea or a shore-side processing plant, can quite often be of better quality than fresh seafood. In order for seafood to be at its best, the fish once dead must go into rigor mortis (the stiffening of the tissue), and then come out of rigor (post rigor). It is at this point that all fish is at its peak of flavor and quality. High-quality fish that is frozen quickly and close to this point in time will thaw to be a wonderful product. Modern factory trawlers have the capability to flash freeze millions of pounds of product. This technique is known as frozen on board. Some of the best quality frozen cod and haddock comes from Iceland, where this technique has been perfected.

An even more high-tech method of freezing that is taking the marketplace by storm is cryogenic freezing. This process freezes fish even faster than blast or flash freezing. Fish flesh is 60 to 70 percent water, and the shorter the freezing time the less damage is done to the cell structure. This means that the quality that goes in is the same level of quality that comes out when thawed properly.

Twenty-five years ago, many customers had a high resistance to purchasing frozen seafood. At that time it was believed that the aging processing of the product could be stopped if it were frozen. Retail operators sometimes may have frozen fresh fish that failed to sell after being on ice for several days. This resulted in poor quality frozen seafood. Freezing took a very long time in store freezers. Once seafood has passed the point of optimum freshness, slow freezing or even fast freezing can only make it worse. Through better education and a more complete understanding of the science of food, merchants have taken a different approach to seafood. Seafood products offered frozen are processed at a proper facility and arrive at the store frozen. To maintain the integrity of their frozen seafood, most retailers will avoid freezing any fish offered as fresh. If it doesn't sell on ice or packaged fresh, it gets thrown out in just a few days. Fresh seafood that has been properly handled and processed will maintain its freshness characteristics for several days. Frozen seafood that has been properly processed and remains solidly frozen will retain good quality for nearly one year.

Which is better, fresh or frozen?

In retail stores today you will find fresh, frozen, and previously frozen seafood. Some frozen products, thawed and sold within that day, provide a very high quality, enjoyable meal. In most of the country, all shrimp sold on ice has been previously frozen (see Chapter 1).

Because of the distance they travel from point of harvest, certain species must arrive frozen to ensure good condition and quality. Orange roughy fillet from New Zealand is one example. Because of seasonality within a certain geographical area, some fish would be unavailable if only sold fresh.

Because of the improvement in the technology and handling of frozen fish, the debate on fresh versus frozen largely comes down to a subjective evaluation of condition. Some retailers take a firm position on fresh versus frozen. They sell only fresh fish, except for shrimp, which, as mentioned earlier, is usually sold previously frozen.

To understand how fresh is fresh, consider the average seafood distribution cycle:

Fish is landed on the boat	day 1
Boat stays out on sea	days 1–5
Boat unloads shore side, fish get processed	days 6–7
Fish is trucked to market, miles away	days 7–8

The point of this example is that much of the fish you buy can easily be 7 to 8 days out of the water before your market gets it. Notice that the term "old" was avoided. The reason is that if fish is properly handled it can maintain a peak of freshness for several more days upon arriving to market. So, sometimes, high-quality frozen seafood thawed just prior to sale, or in your own home when you want it, can be better than fresh. It is the condition of the seafood that counts, whether it is fresh, frozen, or previously frozen.

When evaluating fresh or previously frozen at the market, use the same freshness chart described in the beginning of this chapter for both.

SAFE FOOD HANDLING

Please see **Basic Seafood Facts**, above, for information about the safety of seafood, and for government guidelines on the consumption of raw shellfish.

Pathogenic bacteria that cause disease or illness are usually killed when food is cooked. In many instances, an illness that occurs after eating food is transmitted by a food handler who has touched a cooked food after handling a raw food. This "cross-contamination" can occur with any type of food, including fish and shellfish. You can protect yourself and your family better from food-borne illness from any food by practicing safe food-handling procedures. The FDA recommends four basic steps to food safety:

Clean: Wash your hands often and clean counter surfaces after preparing each food item. Use paper towels instead of sponges or cloths to clean up kitchen surfaces.

Separate: Keep raw meat, poultry, and seafood separate from cooked or ready-to-eat foods in your refrigerator. It is wise to use a different cutting board for raw foods. Always wash hands when they come in contact with raw foods, before handling a cooked food.

Cook: Be sure to cook meats to a proper internal temperature—roasts and steaks to 145 degrees, and poultry to 180 degrees. Fish should be opaque and flake easily. (See **Basic Rules of Seafood Cooking**, below.)

Chill: Keep all perishables refrigerated. Defrost foods gradually in the refrigerator, or under cold running water. Use smaller containers to cool down large quantities of cooked food.

BASIC RULES OF SEAFOOD COOKING

Now that you have a basic knowledge of seafood, where to buy it, how to select it, and how to keep it safe for eating, you can begin to master the recipes in this book. However, to ensure success, it is essential to follow a few basic rules in cooking seafood:

Time it: Seafood cooks fast. Most items take less than 10 minutes. You need to prepare all side dishes first, then cook your seafood. Overcooking is the most frequent cause of a bad meal.

Watch: Stay with the seafood you are cooking. Turn as needed and look for the signs that tell you it is done. Fish turns whitish and firm. Shrimp, lobster, and crab turn red. You can always return seafood to the heat if it is undercooked, so watch it closely.

Thaw: If you are using a frozen seafood item, thaw it before cooking. Allow it to thaw overnight in the refrigerator. Thaw it under cold running water if you need to cook it the same day.

Allow for steaming effect: Cook seafood with moderate heat only. The water inside seafood acts like an internal steamer. Fish removed from the heat slightly undercooked will continue to cook internally as the steam dissipates.

Follow the Canadian cooking rule for seafood: Whatever method of cooking you choose, time your cooking using 10 minutes per inch of thickness. Remove a test piece during cooking and cut into the center of it to see if it is done. If you see a translucent center spot, cook a few more minutes, then remove the food from the heat. As you work with each species group and try the different recipes, your timing for perfect cooking will improve.

COOKING WITH HOT OIL AND BOILING WATER

About oils and shortenings

There are a variety of oils that one can use when cooking seafood: vegetable, corn, olive, peanut, sunflower, and sesame, as well as shortening, butter, and margarine. Which oil works best for each dish is determined by two factors: the degree of heat used, and the flavor aspect of the dish.

High heat oils: Standard vegetable oil mixtures, corn oil, sunflower oil, shortenings, and margarine offer little in terms of flavoring enhancements. These oils are basically used to fry batters, or to inhibit burning or sticking of the food during cooking. For the most part, these oils and shortenings are best used when reaching a maximum temperature of 350 to 375 degrees F.

Flavor-enhancing oils: Olive oil, sesame oil, and peanut oil, as well as butter, are preferred for more delicately balanced dishes. These dishes usually require slower cooking at reduced heat (under 325 degrees F). Such oils tend to burn quickly when used at higher heat ranges.

Maintaining proper cooking temperatures: Introducing cold food into the hot oil will lower the oil temperature, especially when large amounts of food are cooked at one time. Proper temperatures are necessary to ensure rapid cooking without burning, crispness, and minimum absorption of oil. If the food is cooked when the temperature is allowed to drop, the batter often falls off the food and the dish will be unpleasantly greasy. The secrets to maintaining proper cooking temperature are (1) cooking the food in small batches and (2) keeping a close watch on the thermometer.

Safety tips

Many of the precautions necessary to reduce the risk of accidental burning or scalding when using hot oil also apply to cooking with boiling water.

Be careful when placing frozen foods into hot oil. It is best to add frozen foods to hot oil slowly. Large amounts dropped in at one time will cause oil to erupt and possibly overflow the container. Hot oil can ignite and cause fire if it falls onto the burner.

Avoid dripping or spilling water into hot oil. When water comes in contact with hot oil it will cause the oil to pop or explode, sending droplets of hot oil in all directions. Hot oil can burn hands, eyes, and face and can cause fire if it contacts open flames or hot burners.

Always turn handles of pots and pans away from you when cooking with hot oil and boiling water. This will greatly reduce the chance of tipping the pot on yourself and will keep curious children passing by from reaching for handles as well. (When young children are in the house, use back burners in preference to front burners.)

When draining foods cooked in oil it is best to remove food in small quantities to avoid spills. Always drain excess oil from food using a paper towel.

Always turn off burners immediately upon completion of each cooking session with oil or boiling water.

First Aid

For minor burns apply cold running water to burn area. Cooling the burn reduces swelling and draws heat away from the skin. Do not use ice or butter. Once burn area is cooled, apply aloe or first aid burn lotion. Cover the burn loosely with a sterile gauze bandage. Avoid cottony bandages that could stick to skin. Keep the burn area clean and watch for any signs of infection.

For severe burns, contact your physician immediately, or go directly to the emergency room for treatment.

HEALTHY CHOICES: NUTRITIONAL INFORMATION

REDUCING CHOLESTEROL AND HEART DISEASE

Despite fears of ocean pollution and isolated reports of illness associated with eating some fish, there are many good things to say about seafood. A diet that regularly includes finfish and shellfish will help to ensure adequate protein intake. An average serving of finfish provides half the recommended daily allowance of protein for adults. Seafood is low in fat, calories, and sodium, and it is easily digested. Finfish tend to be quite low in cholesterol. Although shellfish was previously reported as being high in cholesterol, after further study it has been found to contain much less than previously thought. According to The National Fisheries Institute *Green Book,* 1997, "Cholesterol in shrimp varies considerably by species, and generally is 1½ to 2 times higher than in the dark meat of chicken, but far less than in eggs."

The omega-3s: good for your heart
Omega-3s are polyunsaturated fatty acids found in fish and shellfish. Finfish high in omega-3s (salmon, mackerel, herring, anchovies, albacore tuna, sardines, striped bass, and bluefish) have been proven to reduce risk of heart attack and strokes. Omega-3s relax arteries and improve circulation, thereby reducing clot formation.

On October 31, 1995, the *Journal of the American Medical Association* reported on a study assessing the cardiac benefits of a type of polyunsaturated fatty acid (long-chain n-3) found primarily in seafood. The study involved a total of 827 subjects aged 24 to 74 years: 334 case patients with primary cardiac arrest attended by paramedics between 1988 and 1994, and 493 population-based controls matched for age and sex. Based on a survey of food intake, the researchers found: "An intake of 5.5 grams of n-3 fatty acids per month was associated with a 50 percent reduction in the risk of primary cardiac arrest."

Another report in *The Journal of the American Medical Association* (January 7, 1998) offers further evidence that fish high in omega-3s are good for your health. The study, which was started in 1982 and compiled eleven years of data, targeted 20,000 middle-aged U.S. male physicians. The results offered promising evidence that for men who consumed fish at least once per week, there were positive health benefits. The study found a 52 percent lower risk of sudden cardiac death for men who ate moderate amounts of fish as a regular part of their diet. Earlier research teams identified fish high in omega-3s to be of most benefit in offering protection against sudden cardiac arrest. However, the new study suggests that even fish that are not high in omega-3s tend to offer similar protection.

NUTRITIONAL INFORMATION ON SEAFOOD

Composition of foods: finfish and shellfish
(100-gram raw edible portion)

SPECIES	Calories (kcal)	Protein (grams)	Total Fat (grams)	Cholesterol (mg)	Sodium (mg)
Shrimp	106	20.31	1.73	152	148
Blue crab	87	18.06	1.08	78	293
Dungeness crab	86	17.46	0.97	59	295
King crab	84	18.29	0.60	42	836
Snow crab	90	18.50	1.18	55	539
Lobster					
American	90	18.80	0.90	95	NA
Spiny	112	20.60	1.51	70	177
Scallops	88	16.78	0.76	33	161
Clams	74	12.77	0.97	34	56
Mussels	86	11.90	2.24	28	286
Oysters					
Eastern	69	7.06	2.47	55	112
Pacific	81	9.45	2.30	NA	106
Conch	75	14.40	1.90	NA	NA
Mahi-mahi	94	19.30	1.10	NA	170

SPECIES	Calories (kcal)	Protein (grams)	Total Fat (grams)	Cholesterol (mg)	Sodium (mg)
Cod					
Atlantic	82	17.81	0.67	43	54
Pacific	82	17.90	0.63	37	71
Flounder	91	18.84	1.19	48	81
Grouper	92	19.38	1.02	37	53
Salmon					
Atlantic	129	18.40	5.60	55	44
Chinook	180	20.06	10.4	66	47
Coho	146	21.62	5.95	39	46
Pink	116	19.94	3.45	52	67
Sockeye	168	21.30	8.56	62	47
Tuna					
Albacore	177	25.30	7.60	NA	40
Bluefin	144	23.33	4.90	38	39
Skipjack	103	22.00	1.01	47	37
Yellowfin	108	23.38	0.95	45	37
Wahoo	124	24.10	2.3	NA	82
Pink snapper	102	21.90	0.9	NA	54
Imitation crab	87	13.00	.65	23	648
Swordfish	121	19.80	4.01	39	90
Halibut	120	22.00	2.0	30	60
Haddock	90	20	1	60	70
Rainbow trout	130	22	4	60	30
Bluefish	124	20	4	59	60
Monkfish	76	15	1	25	18
Skate	89	20	1	NA	90
Tilapia	98	19	2	NA	52
Ocean perch	100	20	2	50	80
Orange roughy	70	16	1	20	70
King fish	105	20	2	53	158
Sea trout	104	17	4	83	58
Striped sea bass	100	20	2	40	65
Sushi, typical serving	70-190	NA	2-3	3-4	70
Smelt	98	19	2	70	60
Abalone	105	77	1	85	301
Crawfish	89	18	1	139	53
Catfish	120	19	1	60	65

Source: *U.S. Department of Agriculture Handbook* 8 (1987).

I

SHRIMP

When supermarket shoppers are asked if they eat seafood, a large number of them say "no." Yet when asked what kind of food they order at a restaurant, many of them reply, "shrimp and lobster." For some reason, consumers don't associate shrimp and lobster with seafood. Of course they know it is seafood, but think of it more as a fun food—a celebration food. This makes sense, because of all the seafood choices, sweet shrimp and tasty lobster are the most popular. Shrimp is America's number one favorite seafood dish. The data prove this: in 1987 the per capita consumption of all forms of shrimp in the United States was 2.3 pounds per person—topped only by canned tuna (5.1 pounds per capita), an inexpensive non-treat protein staple used mainly in sandwiches, salads, and casseroles.

Shrimp is a very easy seafood to prepare in the home. It has a built-in timer. The shell turns red, and the meat becomes snow white when cooked. There are more than 300 species of shrimp harvested for commercial use throughout the world. Species sold in local supermarkets today are arranged by color, size/count per pound, and geographical origin. Knowing the scientific Latin names is unnecessary for you to purchase shrimp, but they are given in this section for those who want to know. Being able to spot the different types at your seafood store is important, however. Size and type determine the price you pay per pound. Most shrimp are sold headless (termed "green headless"), except in Louisiana and Texas, where fresh, head-on shrimp can be successfully rushed to market shortly after harvest.

TYPES OF SHRIMP BY COLOR

The four primary types of shrimp sold in most markets throughout the country are *white, pink, brown,* and *tiger*. In some instances, the color of the white, pink, and brown may look similar. The only true way to distinguish one from the other is by looking at the back of the tail segment. Each color type has special line markings.

White shrimp

The white is considered the premium shrimp in the United States. Most white shrimp *(Penaeus stylirostris, Penaeus vannamei,* and *Penaeus occidentalis)* sold in retail stores are farmed, that is, pond raised. The major producer countries are China *(Penaeus chinensis),* Ecuador, and Peru. There is also a considerable wild harvest off the coast of the Carolinas known as Georgia Whites.

Most white shrimp appears to be grayish to translucent in color. Ecuador white shrimp is by far the restaurant-preferred type for taste and texture. The shrimp are grown in ponds and harvested as they reach a desired market size.

Pink shrimp

Domestic Gulf of Mexico pink shrimp *(Penaeus brevirostris)* is highly regarded as one of the best in Florida and the Gulf states. It is a wild harvest captured primarily in the Tortugas area of the Florida Keys; hence the more common local name, Key West pink shrimp. These shrimp are harvested mostly at night in 35- to 120-foot deep water. The smaller sizes are landed in March and April and the largest sizes in December. Gulf pink shrimp have a sweet flavor and tender texture. There is also a pink shrimp harvest once a year in the cold waters of the North Atlantic; these are commonly called Maine pink shrimp *(Pandalus borealis).*

Brown shrimp

Most commonly known as Texas browns *(Penaeus aztecus),* this type of shrimp is fished from Massachusetts to the Gulf of Mexico. It is wild-harvested in an average water depth of 88 to 170 feet. Brown shrimp provides major tonnage of product throughout the world. The taste is mostly neutral, with a firm texture.

Tiger shrimp

Perhaps the most commonly seen shrimp in supermarkets from coast to coast and north to south is the tiger shrimp *(Penaeus monodon).*

This shrimp is a popular farm-raised species throughout the entire Indo-West Pacific region. Major producing countries are India, Indonesia, Pakistan, Philippines, and Thailand. Wild harvest of tiger shrimp is fished in water depths from shallow to 360 feet. The flavor is sweet and the texture ranges from moderately soft to soft. Today you find this species offered as cooked, tail-on "shrimp cocktail" on the menus of most restaurants.

STANDARD SHRIMP SIZES

You will find shrimp sold either by a descriptive term such as "jumbo" or a count (21/25 count), or both. It is best to purchase your shrimp from a retailer who carries some larger shrimp, at least jumbo 21/25 count. The count is the average number of shrimp you can expect to receive per pound. When displayed side-by-side, shrimp of different sizes may appear to be the same length but will show a noticeable difference in the thickness of the meat. To get your money's worth of shrimp, it is best to know up front just how many shrimp are in the pound. The larger the size, the higher the price. To guide you in your shrimp purchases, use the U.S. Standard Shrimp Grade Chart. This is the accepted standard in the industry. At your store, the count per pound should be in line with this chart. Otherwise, you may be overpaying for shrimp. Shop the markets in your area, and read the weekly circulars. Then compare size and cost to determine which is the best buy.

U.S. Standard Shrimp Grade Chart

DESCRIPTIVE NAME	COUNT PER POUND
EXTRA COLOSSAL	UNDER 10
COLOSSAL	10/15
EXTRA JUMBO	16/20
JUMBO	21/25
EXTRA LARGE	26/30
LARGE	31/35
MEDIUM LARGE	36/42
MEDIUM	43/50
SMALL	51/60
EXTRA SMALL	61/70
TINY	OVER 70

QUALITY

You will always want to purchase your shrimp at a store that has the best quality. Shrimp represents nearly one-third of total seafood sales in the supermarket. This means it sells fast. Since most shrimp offered for sale in stores arrives frozen, you should buy only the shrimp that looks freshly thawed. Ask for your shrimp to be sold to you still frozen if you do not plan to use it immediately, and store it in the freezer.

HOW TO PEEL AND DEVEIN SHRIMP

Some recipes will require that you peel and devein the shrimp before cooking. The "vein" (commonly called the sand vein) runs the full length of the abdomen and is actually not a vein but the intestine of the animal, where waste matter is carried away. Although it is harmless if consumed, most people feel better removing the vein, for it may be dark in color on some shrimp. There is an inexpensive tool that you can buy at the supermarket or any kitchen store called a shrimp deveiner. To peel and devein without a tool, place the thawed shrimp in a bowl of water. Hold shrimp firmly between both index fingers and thumbs and bend back and forth to snap the back of the shell at the center. Now with one hand, hold the meaty end firmly and pinch the tail section and pull it with the index finger and thumb of the other hand. This should strip away the tail section. Next, pull the shell away from the remainder of the body by pulling off legs and shell. Lay the peeled shrimp on its side and with a small paring knife cut a shallow V along the back and remove the sand vein. Rinse and prepare to cook.

A note on shrimp sizes used in recipes:

In these recipes, you may select the size and type of shrimp that please you best. The size listed in the recipe is just a suggestion taking into consideration that larger sizes are easier to peel and devein. Smaller sizes are suggested for bisque and Creole dishes.

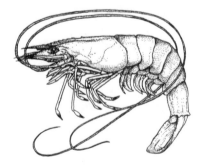

BASIC PEEL-AND-EAT STEAMED SHRIMP, MARYLAND STYLE

1 pound shell-on shrimp, 36/40 count or larger
¼ cup white distilled vinegar
2 tablespoons Old Bay Seasoning or seafood seasoning
½ cup ketchup
½ teaspoon horseradish
¼ lemon
¼ teaspoon hot sauce

Choose a pot large enough to allow a colander to rest a few inches above the bottom. Add hot tap water to a depth of 2 inches. Add white distilled vinegar. (Vinegar helps to create a more dense steam.) Place colander in pot. Bring liquid to a boil, and spread thawed shrimp in the colander. Sprinkle the shrimp with Old Bay Seasoning. Cover pot and cook for 2 minutes. Uncover; remove one shrimp; cut in half with a knife to check for full white, cottony color throughout. If done, remove from heat and serve hot. Peel and eat. Serve with homemade cocktail sauce.

Cocktail sauce: Mix ketchup, horseradish, squeeze of lemon, and hot sauce in a small cup or glass and serve.
SERVES 2.

EASY SHRIMP SCAMPI TO DIE FOR

1 pound shell-on shrimp, 36/40 count or larger
½ stick sweet butter
½ bunch fresh scallions, finely chopped
1 teaspoon garlic, crushed or freshly chopped

Peel, devein, and rinse shrimp. Heat a medium-sized non-stick skillet to medium/high meat. Add butter, scallions, and garlic, and stir constantly until golden. Turn heat to high, add shrimp, and stir for 2 minutes until all shrimp have turned red. Check one shrimp to see if it is cooked. If done, remove scampi from heat and serve.
SERVES 2.

SIDE DISH SUGGESTIONS: Baked potato, carrots, and a crusty French bread for dipping in scampi sauce. (Note: potato and carrots should be fully cooked before cooking scampi.)

BASIC QUICK-BOILED SHRIMP, NEW ORLEANS STYLE

1 pound shell-on shrimp, 36/40 count or larger
1 packet Louisiana Shrimp and Crab Boil
  or mixture of 3 crushed bay leaves, 1 tablespoon mustard
  seed, ½ teaspoon celery salt, ¼ teaspoon red pepper, ¼
  teaspoon black pepper, sprinkle of coriander. (Get a
  Cry-O-Vac bakery bag from the supermarket bakery, the
  kind with the tiny holes in it. Put the mixture in the bag,
  and tie it closed.)

Peel, devein, and rinse shrimp. Choose a one-quart pot. Fill to ¾ full
with hot tap water and bring to a boil. Add one packet of Louisiana
Shrimp and Crab Boil (or mixture). Add shrimp to boiling water. Cook
for two minutes. Remove shrimp, check center for proper cooking (meat
should be white and opaque). If cooked to your satisfaction, remove from
pot and serve hot with cocktail sauce (see **Basic Peel-and-Eat Shrimp,
Maryland Style**, page 27).
SERVES 2.

BACON-WRAPPED BBQ SHRIMP WITH MONTEREY JACK CHEESE

1 pound shell-on shrimp, 21/25 count or larger
8 to 10 strips of bacon
¼ cup BBQ sauce
¼ pound Monterey Jack cheese

Pre-heat the broiler. Peel, devein, and rinse shrimp. Pre-cook strips of
bacon in microwave or skillet until nearly done. Cut cheese into small
slices, one for each shrimp. Cut bacon strips into halves or thirds
(allowing one for each shrimp). Wrap bacon around shrimp. Brush
with BBQ sauce. Place bacon-wrapped BBQ shrimp on broiler tray
(position tray on top shelf nearest heat). Cook for 3 minutes. Remove
the broiler tray from heat. Place a slice of cheese over each shrimp,
brush with BBQ sauce. Return to heat for one minute to melt cheese.
Serve hot. (This recipe can also be prepared on the outside grill using a
flat, non-stick perforated fish pan.)
SERVES 4 to 6.
SIDE DISH SUGGESTIONS: Potato salad and baked beans.

FAST AND EASY BUTTERFLY SHRIMP FRY

1 pound shell-on shrimp, 16-20 count
1 cup flour
1 tablespoon Old Bay Seasoning or seafood seasoning
½ teaspoon salt
1 egg
¼ cup milk
¼ cup olive or other vegetable oil

Peel, devein, and rinse shrimp. To butterfly, use sharp knife to cut shrimp head to tail, ¾ of the way through the back. Mix flour, Old Bay Seasoning, and salt on a large piece of wax paper. Beat egg with milk until yellow. Place butterfly shrimp in egg wash for 5 minutes. Select a large non-stick skillet, add oil, and pre-heat on medium heat. Remove shrimp from egg wash; spread open gently to butterfly and pat each shrimp one by one in flour mixture to get a good coating. Then place in hot skillet. The shrimp will begin to turn red on the underside almost immediately. Cook about 1 to 1½ minutes. Turn shrimp and cook 1 to 1½ minutes more. Break one shrimp in half to test for doneness. If done, remove shrimp from skillet and place on paper towel to drain excess oil.
SERVES 3.
SIDE DISH SUGGESTIONS: Coleslaw and French fries.

PERFECT COCKTAIL SHRIMP

1 pound shell-on shrimp, 36/40 count or larger

Peel, devein, and rinse shrimp. Fill a one-quart pot ¾ full of hot tap water and bring to a boil. Add shrimp to boiling water and cook for two minutes. Remove one shrimp and check center for proper cooking (meat should be white and opaque). If cooked to your satisfaction, remove shrimp from water and **immediately** chill down by rinsing shrimp under cold running water, then bury in a bowl of ice. Cold water and ice stop the internal cooking process and give the shrimp a nice snappy cocktail crunch. (See **Basic Peel-and-Eat Steamed Shrimp, Maryland Style,** page 27, for a simple cocktail sauce recipe.)
SERVES 2.
SIDE DISH SUGGESTION: Freshly cut peeled carrots and celery stalks.

SHRIMP CREOLE

1 pound raw frozen salad shrimp, peeled and deveined
2 fresh red bell peppers
2 fresh green bell peppers
1 large onion
½ cup chopped celery
1 clove chopped garlic
2 tablespoons olive oil
1 1-pound can crushed tomatoes
1 8-ounce can tomato sauce
1 teaspoon cayenne pepper
1½ teaspoon black pepper
1 teaspoon chili powder
1 teaspoon salt
1 teaspoon sugar
3 tablespoons flour
¼ cup water

Chop peppers, onion, celery, and garlic. Thaw and rinse shrimp. Select a 6-quart pot, add oil and pre-heat on medium heat. Stir in chopped vegetables and cook until colors turn bright and food is tender. Add crushed tomatoes, tomato sauce, cayenne pepper, black pepper, chili powder, salt, and sugar. Cover and cook for 20 minutes. Add shrimp and continue to cook for 3 minutes. Whisk flour and water in a cup and stir slowly into creole to thicken.
SERVES 4 to 6.
SIDE DISH SUGGESTIONS: Yellow rice and black beans.

CHINESE SHRIMP AND BROCCOLI

1 pound shell-on shrimp, 36/40 count or smaller
1 stalk fresh broccoli
3 tablespoons vegetable oil
2 tablespoons soy sauce
3 tablespoons oyster sauce
3 tablespoons water

Chinese cooking requires speed and attention to avoid overcooking. (Steam your rice ahead of time.) Peel, devein, and rinse shrimp. Cut broccoli into florets. Split stems into thin slices. Fill a one-quart pot ¾ full of water and place on high heat. As soon as water reaches a boil,

add broccoli, and cook only until it blooms to a rich shiny green (about 1 to 1½ minutes). Remove from water and drain. Select a wok or deep skillet, add oil and place on high heat. Add shrimp, and stir until red (about 2 minutes). Mix in broccoli; add soy sauce, oyster sauce, and water. Using two spatulas, lift the food off the heat continuously until entire meal is heated. Remove from heat and serve.
SERVES 2 to 4.
SIDE DISH SUGGESTIONS: White rice or chicken and rice soup.

EASY SHRIMP PIZZA WITH MUSHROOMS

1 pound shell-on shrimp, 41/50 count or larger
1 teaspoon yeast
¼ cup vegetable oil
1 cup warm tap water
3 cups flour
vegetable spray
1 14-ounce can or jar pizza sauce
2 tablespoons grated Parmesan cheese
1 tablespoon garlic, chopped
1 cup fresh mushrooms, sliced
8 ounces mozzarella cheese, shredded

In a deep bowl combine yeast, oil, and water and let stand for 5 minutes. Gradually add flour and mix until dough is elastic but not gummy. If too wet, add more flour. Form dough into a ball. Spray a deep bowl with vegetable spray and place dough inside; then cover with towel and let rest to rise for 30 minutes. Peel, devein, and rinse shrimp. Pre-heat the oven to 425 degrees F. When dough has risen, spread flour over table and roll out dough until ¹⁄₁₆ inch thick. Place dough in oiled 16-inch pizza pan or cornmeal-dusted pizza stone. Add sauce and Parmesan cheese and bake for 10 minutes. With 2 tablespoons heated oil in a skillet, stir-fry shrimp, garlic, and mushrooms until shrimp is cooked, about 3 minutes. Remove pizza from oven. Sprinkle shrimp/mushroom mixture over pizza. Sprinkle mozzarella cheese over top, return to oven and cook until cheese is golden. Slice and serve.
SERVES 4 to 6.

STUFFED BAKED SHRIMP

1 pound shell-on shrimp, 16/25 count or larger
8 ounces blue crab or snow crab meat
¼ cup butter
¼ cup celery, finely chopped
¼ cup onion, finely chopped
1 egg
¼ teaspoon mayonnaise
¼ teaspoon mustard
¼ teaspoon Old Bay Seasoning or seafood seasoning
3 soda crackers, crushed

Pre-heat the oven to 450 degrees F. Melt butter in a skillet; add celery and onion and cook until soft. In a bowl, mix egg, mayonnaise, mustard, Old Bay Seasoning, crab meat, celery, onion, and cracker. Place in refrigerator to chill. Peel, devein, butterfly, and rinse shrimp. (To butterfly, use sharp knife to cut shrimp head to tail, through back ¾ of the way through.) Place one tablespoon stuffing on each shrimp. Place shrimp in a baking pan or dish and bake for 10 minutes. Brush tops of shrimp with butter and broil just enough to brown top of stuffing.
SERVES 3 to 4.
SIDE DISH SUGGESTIONS: Long grain wild rice and French style string beans.

BLACKENED SHRIMP

1 pound shell-on shrimp, 41/50 count or larger
¼ cup melted butter
¼ cup blackened seafood seasoning or Cajun seasoning

Note: Blackened dishes require fast cooking at very high heat. Be sure to select a skillet that can withstand high temperature, preferably a black iron skillet.

Peel, devein, and rinse shrimp. (Shrimp can also be cooked shell-on.) Pre-heat skillet at high heat for about 2 minutes. Dip shrimp in melted butter. Spread seasoning on wax paper and pat shrimp into seasoning on both sides. Immediately place in skillet and cook until seasoning turns black, approximately 3 minutes. Remove from heat and serve.
SERVES 3 to 4.
SIDE DISH SUGGESTIONS: Tangy cucumber salad and yellow rice.

GRILLED-BBQ PEEL-AND-EAT SHRIMP

1 pound shell-on shrimp, 36/40 count or larger
½ cup BBQ sauce

Note: Smaller sizes of shrimp may fall through grates of grill. If you plan to cook seafood on the grill regularly, purchase a perforated Teflon seafood grill pan found at any kitchen store.

Pre-heat the grill. Marinate shrimp in bowl with BBQ sauce. Place shrimp on grill. Cook one side about 2 minutes, turn, baste with BBQ sauce, and cook for 2 minutes. Remove from grill and serve hot. SERVES 2.
SIDE DISH SUGGESTIONS: Baked beans, potato salad, and grilled, toasted French bread.

SHRIMP TEMPURA WITH CRUNCHY VEGGIES

1 pound shell-on shrimp, 26/30 count or larger
3 fresh carrots
1 squash
1 broccoli stalk
4 eggs
¼ teaspoon salt
¼ teaspoon sugar
2¼ cups flour
4 cups vegetable oil
2 cups Japanese or other bread crumbs (Japanese bread
crumbs can be found in Asian markets)

Peel, devein, and rinse shrimp (leaving tails attached). Skin carrots and cut into thin strips. Slice squash thin. Cut off stem of broccoli, leaving just the florets. Beat eggs, salt, and sugar and gradually add flour. Heat oil in deep pot at medium heat. Dip vegetables in batter and then roll thoroughly in bread crumbs. Place in hot oil. (Oil temperature should be 320 to 350 degrees F.) Cook vegetables until bread crumbs turn golden. Remove vegetables from oil and allow excess oil to drain onto paper towel. Rinse shrimp, dip in batter, and roll thoroughly in bread crumbs. Place battered shrimp in hot oil. Cook until golden brown (about 5 minutes). SERVES 3 to 4.
SIDE DISH SUGGESTION: Steamed rice.

SPICY SHRIMP FAJITA

  1 pound shell-on shrimp, any size
  1 large sweet onion
  2 carrots
  2 tablespoons butter
  ¼ cup soy sauce
  1 tablespoon brown sugar
  1 teaspoon vinegar
  1 14-ounce package of burrito style or fajita tortilla wraps

Peel, devein, and rinse shrimp. Slice onion; peel carrots and slice into thin strips. Pre-heat a large skillet at medium heat. Combine butter, shrimp, onions, and carrots. Mix soy sauce, sugar, and vinegar. Pour liquid over shrimp and vegetables and then stir-fry for 5 minutes. Place tortillas in microwave to warm. Remove shrimp mixture from stove, spoon into tortilla wraps, and roll.
SERVES 3 to 4.
SIDE DISH SUGGESTION: Yellow rice.

SWEET AND SOUR PEPPER SHRIMP

  1 pound shell-on shrimp, 36/40 count or larger
  1 sweet bell pepper
  1 onion
  3 tablespoons oil
  ¼ cup tomato paste
  ¼ cup brown sugar
  ¼ cup vinegar
  1 cup water
  3 teaspoons cornstarch

Remove seeds from bell pepper, and then slice pepper and onion into strips. Peel, devein, and rinse shrimp. Add oil, shrimp, peppers, and onions and stir-fry at medium heat until shrimp is cooked (check center of one shrimp; meat should be white). Add sweet and sour sauce to skillet and cook for 1 minute.

Sweet and sour sauce: Combine tomato paste, sugar, vinegar, water, and cornstarch in saucepan and bring to boil at medium heat. Boil for one minute and stir continuously. Remove from heat.
SERVES 3 to 4.
SIDE DISH SUGGESTION: Steamed rice.

SHRIMPY TOAST

4 ounces frozen cooked salad shrimp
2 eggs
¼ cup milk
2 scallions, chopped
¼ teaspoon salt
¼ teaspoon pepper
2 tablespoons flour
1 cup vegetable oil
4 slices bread

Thaw and rinse shrimp. Puree the shrimp, eggs, milk, scallions, salt, pepper, and flour in a blender for 5 seconds. In a skillet, heat oil to 350 degrees F. Pour shrimp batter into a large bowl. Dip bread into batter, coating both sides. Fry until golden, 1 or 2 minutes. Drain on paper towel. Cut bread into quarters.

SERVES 3 to 4.

SIDE DISH SUGGESTION: Fried Chinese noodles with sweet and sour sauce.

SESAME HONEY BBQ SHRIMP

1 pound shell-on shrimp, 36/40 count or larger
1 egg
¼ cup milk
2 cups flour
2 cups vegetable oil
¼ cup honey
¼ cup BBQ sauce
1 tablespoon sesame seeds

Peel, devein, and rinse shrimp. In a deep bowl mix egg, milk, and shrimp. Let stand for 5 minutes. Remove shrimp and roll in flour. In a skillet heat oil to 375 degrees F. Fry shrimp until golden brown, about 3 minutes. Remove from heat. Drain oil from skillet; add honey, BBQ sauce and sesame seeds. Cook on medium low heat for 1 minute. Stir in shrimp quickly, cook for 1 minute only and then remove from heat and serve.

SERVES: 2 to 4.

SIDE DISH SUGGESTIONS: Sweet corn and cucumber slices.

HIBACHI SHRIMP TERIYAKI WITH VEGETABLES

1 pound shell-on shrimp, 16/20 count or larger
2 yellow squash
2 sweet yellow or red bell peppers
½ pound large fresh mushrooms
2 large sweet onions
1 cup teriyaki sauce
1 teaspoon brown sugar
vegetable spray

Peel, devein, and rinse shrimp. Cut squash and peppers into large strips. Wash mushrooms to remove soil. Peel onions and cut into quarters. Place shrimp, squash, onion, mushrooms, and peppers in a large bowl. Mix teriyaki sauce and sugar. Pour liquid over veggies and shrimp, and marinate for 5 minutes. Pre-heat the hibachi or grill. (Use a perforated Teflon seafood pan or aluminum foil if grilling.) Spray hibachi or grill pan with vegetable spray. Place all ingredients on hibachi and continuously turn gently. Pour remaining teriyaki sauce over shrimp and veggies as they cook. Total cooking time should be about 3 to 5 minutes. Remove from heat and serve hot.
SERVES 2 to 4.
SIDE DISH SUGGESTIONS: Hot tea and steamed white rice.

MEDITERRANEAN SHRIMP MEDLEY

1 pound any size shell-on shrimp
½ pound angel hair pasta
1 stalk broccoli
½ bunch scallions
1 10½-ounce can white clam sauce

Peel, devein, and rinse shrimp. Cook pasta in boiling water, following directions on box. Rinse pasta with cold water and set aside. In a medium saucepan, boil shrimp for only 3 minutes. Remove from heat and set aside. Cut broccoli and scallions into small bite-sized pieces and boil until colors turn vivid green. Remove from heat and drain. In a large skillet heat clam sauce and vegetables for 4 minutes at medium heat. Place pasta in shallow bowls, spoon clam and vegetable mixture over pasta, and garnish with cooked shrimp.
SERVES 2 to 4.
SIDE DISH SUGGESTIONS: Crusty Italian bread and slices of fresh tomato.

DEEP-FRIED BUFFALO SHRIMP

1 pound shell-on shrimp, 36/40 count or larger
2 cups vegetable oil
1 egg
¼ cup milk
2 cups flour
1 teaspoon salt
½ cup butter
½ cup hot sauce
6 celery stalks
¼ cup horseradish
1 tablespoon mayonnaise

Peel, devein and rinse shrimp. Pre-heat oil in a medium-sized pot. In a
bowl, beat egg with milk. Mix flour and salt on a large sheet of wax
paper. Dip shrimp in liquid and then roll in flour. Re-dip shrimp in
liquid and roll once more in flour. Place shrimp in hot oil and deep fry
until golden, about 3 to 5 minutes. Remove shrimp from oil and drain
on paper towel. Combine butter and hot sauce in a small bowl and
microwave for 30 seconds or until butter is melted; pour sauce over
shrimp. Slice celery into strips. Combine horseradish and mayonnaise
for a dipping sauce. Cut celery stalks into 4- to 6-inch pieces. (Celery
can be eaten to reduce burning in mouth from hot sauce.)
SERVES: 4 to 6.

See also:
Classic Shrimp Salad, page 148
Shrimp and Fresh Fruit Salad, page 147
Shrimp and Imitation Crabmeat Platter, page 177
Shrimp Party Platter, page 178
Three-Step Best Darm Chunky Shrimp Bisque, page 139

▐▌

CRAB

Imagine the first person on earth ever to eat a crab—the first person who watched a bird capture a crab, dash it across the rocks, and make a meal of it. The first person to eat a crab was probably very hungry and ate it as the bird did—raw. Cooking crab must have been a sublime discovery. Crab is not the prettiest species of seafood, but oh how wonderful they taste when cooked just right!

This chapter will cover the most common crabs sold throughout the country. People who live in coastal states have their own crabbing stories and favorite family recipes. On the East Coast, from New York to Florida, they tie a raw chicken neck on a long string, sling it into the bay or river, and wait. One person slowly pulls in the string while another waits anxiously with the net. When a big crab is seen clutching the chicken neck, you can usually hear a shout down the pier, "Get the net!" Then they take their catch of the day home, steam them in Old Bay Seasoning, or add them to mom's best marinara sauce.

In Florida, in the Gulf of Mexico, they bait the stone crabs into a basket, snap off the claws and throw the crab back to sea. The crab grows two new claws in about 18 months. It's no surprise that stone crab claws are expensive.

Crabmeat is considered to be the most delicate, sweetest-flavored seafood of all. Why else would folks sit for hours and pick the meat from these tiny crustaceans? There are five popular species: blue crab, king crab, snow crab, stone crab, and Dungeness crab. They range in length from a few inches for most to as wide as a young boy can spread his arms (king crab). The crab is in the family known as *Crustacea,* meaning shellfish that has an external skeleton and jointed legs. Crabs are bottom feeders and eat anything that doesn't eat them first. As they increase in size they slip out of their shell and grow a larger one.

The nice thing about working with crab is that you can use the meat from any species in any crab recipe. The taste may change somewhat, but the sweet flavor of crab makes any dish a treat.

GETTING TO KNOW CRAB

Blue crab

These bluish crabs are found along the entire Atlantic seaboard, in bays and salty rivers. Customers buy them alive as hard or soft-shell, steamed, or cooked in cans. The soft-shell is a blue crab that has just molted (grown a new shell). Females molt 18 to 23 times in a lifetime, whereas males molt all their lives. While the crab is soft, crab lovers clean the animal, batter it lightly, and gently fry in butter. It can then be served on bread, with lettuce and fresh tomato; the entire shell, claws and legs are eaten. Hard-shell crabs are cooked alive by steaming with spice or garlic or in a sweet home-made pasta sauce. Typical eating crabs range from 4½ to 7 inches across the shell. The catch is best in warm summer months and year-round in the Gulf of Mexico.

King crab

You will find these monstrous crabs in the northwest Pacific and Bering Sea area from Alaska to Japan. The king crab has an average weight of about 8 pounds. The catch is seasonal and on a quota system. Red king crabs grow up to nearly 7 feet from the tip of one leg to the other. Most king crab is sold cooked, in leg and claw portions. King crab commands a high price due to its highly rich, succulent taste.

Snow crab

There are two seasons for this crab. One is the Alaskan, which takes place in early winter in the Bering Sea. The second season, called the Canadian, begins in early spring and occurs in the North Atlantic. Of the two producing areas, it is the Alaskan catch that has the superior taste and texture. These crabs can average up to 5 pounds each. Snow crab is traditionally sold cooked, in "clusters"—that is, split into two parts, each consisting of a body section, a claw, and four legs. Of the five most popular crabs, snow crab gives the most meat for the price.

Stone crab

Indigenous to the Gulf of Mexico, these crabs are harvested only for their claws. The claws are removed and the crab is thrown back into the water where it grows new claws. Stone crabs have a very hard shell, somewhat like porcelain. The tips of the claws are jet black. The rest of the claw is white and the topside turns red when cooked. The average size of the crab is about 5 inches point-to-point. The claws weigh an average of 4 ounces or more. Visitors to Florida look forward to enjoying stone crab claws at their favorite restaurants. While the season is long, October to May, most of the local catch is made in the early fall.

Dungeness crab

These crabs are caught from September to February on the Northwest Coast, and are the favorite of many crab fanciers. High demand on the West Coast means that most of the catch stays west of the Mississippi River. One crab can reach a weight of nearly 4 pounds, with a minimum legal shell size for capture of 6¼ inches point-to-point. These crabs are very meaty and easy to pick. Dungeness crabs are sold whole cooked, and in 5-pound blocks of frozen meat.

CLEANING CRABS

Snow crab, king crab, and stone crab arrive at market pre-cooked. Sold as legs, clusters, or claws, they require no cleaning; the meat is removed from the shell and eaten. The blue crab and Dungeness crab are most often sold whole, raw or cooked, and need to be cleaned before being eaten.

To clean a crab, turn it on its back, with legs up. With the point of a knife or your finger, pull the apron tab—the V-shaped tab in the middle of the under body—up and off. Next turn the crab over and place your finger or knife (blade facing away from you) into the opening in the shell where the apron was removed, and pull the top shell off. Using a knife or your fingers, scrape or pull off the six grayish, hair-like pointed gills on each side of the body and discard them. (Experienced crab pickers refer to the gills as "the dead man.") Finally, break off the eyes and mouth area and discard them. In between the two body sections you will find material that will be green, yellowish, and red in color. This is the heart and fat of the animal. Many consider it to be a tasty delicate treat. It is perfectly safe to consume, but to do so is purely a matter of personal taste.

SOUTHERN STEAMED BLUE CRAB—
SPICY, GARLIC, OR BBQ

> 2 dozen live blue crabs (snow crabs may be substituted)
> ¼ cup white distilled vinegar
> 2 cups water
> ¼ cup Old Bay Seasoning, or other seafood seasoning, dry
> garlic powder, or dry BBQ powder

Pour water and vinegar into a deep soup stockpot or crab/clam pot with a steamer insert. Place a curved piece of chicken wire or colander upside down over the pot so that crabs will stay out of the liquid. Place a layer of crab over the steamer insert and sprinkle with seasoning; add another layer and repeat until pot is full. Cover, turn heat to high, and steam for approximately 30 minutes until crab turns red. (If using snow crab, the cooking time will be 5 minutes, since snow crabs are sold pre-cooked.) Remove crab from heat. Serve hot. Provide a wooden crab mallet to crack claws.

SERVES 6 to 8.

SIDE DISH SUGGESTIONS: Cold drinks, cornbread, and potato salad.

BOILED PACIFIC SNOW CRAB OR KING CRAB

2 1-pound snow crab clusters or king crab legs
½ cup melted butter

This is one of the easiest seafood dishes to prepare in the home. Select a soup stockpot, 6 quarts or larger, and fill ¾ full with hot tap water. Place on high heat. Rinse crab under cold water to remove brine. When water reaches a hard boil, place crab in pot and boil for 3 minutes. (These crabs are pre-cooked and only need to be heated.) Remove crab from pot, and serve with hot drawn butter.

Snow crab shells are thin. The best way to remove the meat is to use your fingers to snap off one end of the leg, then place a prong of a fork inside the leg and push it up the leg to split the shell. King shells are hard, and they have sharp spines, which protect the animal from predators in the wild. You will need to use a crab mallet or nutcracker to break the shell.

SERVES 4 to 6.

SIDE DISH SUGGESTIONS: Fresh tossed salad, crusty French bread.

LIGHT BUTTER-FRIED SOFT CRAB SANDWICH

4 medium to large soft blue crabs (fresh or frozen)
1 egg
¼ cup milk
1 teaspoon salt, or to taste
1 teaspoon pepper, or to taste
½ stick butter
1 cup flour
1 fresh tomato, sliced
4 leaves of lettuce
2 tablespoons mayonnaise
8 slices white or whole wheat bread

Clean crabs by gently turning point of shell on each side toward center. With a knife, cut away the six gray lungs. Turn crab upside down, remove apron tab, and cut away eyes and mouth with one slice. Mix egg, milk, salt, and pepper. Pre-heat skillet with butter on medium heat. Dip crab into batter; gently roll in flour and fry until golden brown. Serve on soft bread with slices of tomato, lettuce, and mayonnaise. Note: Since crab is soft, the entire shell, including legs and claws, is to be eaten.

SERVES 4.

DUNGENESS CRAB, CALIFORNIA STYLE

4 live Dungeness crabs (or 1 crab per person)
½ cup butter
1 packet crab/shrimp boil (see **Basic Quick Boiled Shrimp**, page 27)

Select a pot 6 quarts or larger. Fill ¾ with hot tap water. Add crab/shrimp seasoning bag and bring to a boil. Place live crabs in pot and cook until shells turn bright red (about 10 minutes). Remove crabs from pot and serve hot with melted butter. Dungeness crabs are cleaned the same way as blue crab. (See above.)

SERVES 4.

SIDE DISH SUGGESTIONS: Fresh cucumber salad and bread sticks.

CHESAPEAKE BAY TRADITIONAL CRAB CAKES

1 pound blue crab meat (other crabmeat may be substituted)
2 slices dry bread
1 teaspoon Old Bay Seasoning
1 teaspoon baking soda
1 egg
2 tablespoon mayonnaise
1 tablespoon Worcestershire sauce
1 teaspoon dry or wet mustard
2 cups flour
1½ cups vegetable oil

Check the crabmeat for shells and place it in a large bowl. Crumble dry bread over crabmeat. Sprinkle Old Bay Seasoning and baking soda over crabmeat. In a small bowl whisk egg, mayonnaise, Worcestershire sauce, and mustard. Pour liquid over crabmeat and mix gently with hands. Shape into tight, round, medium-lemon-sized balls or cakes 2 inches wide. Place flour on a large sheet of wax paper, and roll each crab ball or cake into flour. Add oil to skillet, place on medium heat, and fry crab cakes until golden. Turn as needed. (The only raw ingredient in the recipe is the egg. Cooking time needs to be long enough just to brown cake and heat inside).

SERVES 4.

SIDE DISH SUGGESTION: Serve on saltine crackers, or as an entrée with corn-on-the-cob and fresh slices of tomato.

DEVILED CRAB

  1 pound cooked crabmeat, any type
  ¼ cup onion, finely chopped
  ¼ cup celery, finely chopped
  ½ cup sweet bell pepper, finely chopped
  1 tablespoon fresh parsley, finely chopped
  ¼ cup butter
  ½ cup mayonnaise
  1 tablespoon lemon juice
  1 teaspoon dry or wet mustard
  ¼ cup heavy cream
  1 teaspoon Worcestershire sauce
  1 cup salted crackers, crushed
  1 teaspoon cayenne pepper, or to taste

Preheat oven to 400 degrees F. Sauté onion, celery, sweet pepper, and parsley in small skillet with butter at low heat until soft. Mix in all remaining ingredients with crushed crackers and vegetables. Place in a medium casserole dish and bake until top is browned (about 25 minutes).

SERVES 3 to 5.

SIDE DISH SUGGESTIONS: Stir-fried zucchini and button mushrooms.

CRABMEAT OMELET, WESTERN STYLE

  8 ounces special blue crabmeat or other crab as available
  1 green bell pepper
  1 medium onion
  1 tablespoon butter
  4 eggs
  ¼ cup milk
  2 dashes Tabasco sauce
  1 teaspoon paprika

Chop pepper and onion into fine pieces. In a medium-sized non-stick skillet, melt butter at medium heat. Sauté onion and pepper until soft. Beat eggs, milk, and Tabasco sauce until creamy yellow and pour over vegetables. Allow omelet to cook on bottom until firm, sprinkle with crabmeat and fold in half. Cook until omelet is firm. Sprinkle with paprika and serve.

SERVES 2 TO 4.

SIDE DISH SUGGESTIONS: Home fries and buttered biscuits.

BALTIMORE STYLE CRAB IMPERIAL

1 pound lump crabmeat from backfin
2 tablespoons butter
¼ cup milk
1 tablespoon flour
1 teaspoon salt, or to taste
1 teaspoon pepper, or to taste
½ small onion, minced
2 slices bread
¼ teaspoon Worcestershire sauce
½ teaspoon lemon juice
¼ cup mayonnaise
vegetable spray
1 tablespoon paprika

Melt butter in a skillet at low heat. Stir flour into milk and add to skillet with salt, pepper, minced onion, and bread, crumbled. Bring to medium heat, stirring constantly, and cook until thickened. Pre-heat oven to 350 degrees F. Remove sauce from stove; add crabmeat, Worcestershire sauce, lemon juice, and mayonnaise. Gently fold in crab mixture. Spray glass baking dish with vegetable spray. Fill with crab imperial mixture, sprinkle top with paprika, and bake for 10 to 12 minutes until top turns golden.

SERVES 3 to 4.

SIDE DISH SUGGESTIONS: Wild rice with long-grain rice and salad.

FLORIDA STONE CRAB CLAWS, SPICY OR BUTTERY

2 pounds stone crab claws
½ cup butter or spicy mustard

Fill a 6-quart or larger pot ¾ full with hot tap water. Place on high heat. When water reaches a hard boil, place crab claws in pot and boil for 3 minutes. (These crabs are pre-cooked and only need to be heated.) Melt ½ cup of butter (or serve with spicy mustard instead). Remove crab from pot and serve. Provide a crab mallet to crack claws. The claws are very hard and may be purchased from the store scored (split on one side) to make opening easier.

SERVES 4 to 5.

SIDE DISH SUGGESTION: Boiled potatoes in garlic butter.

CRAB AND MUSHROOM QUICHE

    6 ounces crabmeat (any type)
    1 9-inch frozen deep-dish pie shell
    3 fresh scallions, finely chopped
    1 cup mushrooms, thinly sliced
    1 tablespoon butter
    2 tablespoons flour
    1 cup whole milk
    1 tablespoon mayonnaise
    3 eggs, beaten
    1 cup Swiss cheese, chunked small

Pre-heat the oven to 400 degrees F. Poke two small holes in bottom of pie shell and bake for 5 minutes. Remove shell from heat and set aside. Sauté scallions and mushrooms in small skillet with butter for 3 minutes. In a mixing bowl whisk flour, milk, and mayonnaise. Add beaten eggs and whisk until creamy. Stir in crabmeat, sautéed vegetables, and cheese chunks. Pour quiche batter into pie shell and bake for 40 to 45 minutes. Remove from oven and let cool for 5 to 10 minutes to allow pie to set. Slice and serve.

SERVES 6 to 8.

SIDE DISH SUGGESTION: Fresh fruit slices.

See also:

Baked Mid-Atlantic Bluefish with Crabmeat Stuffing, page 118
Bird's Nest Cajun Crab Dip, page 174
Classic Crab-Stuffed Lobster, page 51
Crab and Cheese Party Dip, page 173
Flounder Stuffed with Crabmeat, page 105
Fried Crab Balls, page 176
Hearty Crab Bisque, page 140
Maryland Style Crab Soup, page 140
Spinach and Garlic Crab Balls, page 176
Stuffed Mushroom Caps, page 181

LOBSTER

In a good restaurant one of the main entrees on the menu will usually be lobster. One of the top meals requested by mom on Mother's Day is lobster. Everyone loves lobster. Many of us have grown up experiencing lobster as a special treat. When you're invited out to dinner and told to order whatever you wish, the answer is often, "I'll have the lobster."

AMERICAN LOBSTER

In the United States, consumption of lobster has risen steadily through the years. Most lobster comes from Maine. More than 35 million pounds are produced from its cold ocean coastline annually. The American lobster (*Homarus americanus*) is mostly sold live. It has two claws, one large with hard molar-like teeth, the other smaller and flat with razor-like teeth. When the lobster captures prey, it holds the fish with the large claw squeezing it tightly. The other claw rips the food and delivers it to the lobster's mouth. Hence, the big claw is called the "crusher" and the small one the "ripper."

When you see lobsters at your supermarket or fish store, you will notice that they have rubber bands on their claws. Many people believe these are put on the lobster so the customer will be safe from the claw. The truth is that lobsters are cannibalistic. If they are hungry and fail to find suitable food, they will consume each other. One lobster in a tank free of banded claws will snack on an entire lobster overnight.

American lobsters can live for many years in the wild. Some have been captured that are believed to be over 140 years old. How can the fishermen tell the age of a lobster? It takes 7 years for a lobster to grow one pound. The largest lobsters ever caught in the North Atlantic have been over 20 pounds. Although fished year round, nearly three-quarters of the annual catch is taken from summer through fall.

SPINY LOBSTER

The most widely fished species are known as spiny lobsters (*Panulirus spp.* and *Jasus spp*). They are caught in the Florida Keys, the Caribbean, off the western coast of Mexico, and off the coasts South America, South Africa, Oman, Yemen, Australia, and New Zealand. Spiny lobsters have no claws. They are shipped live world wide, but in the United States frozen tails are more common.

Spiny lobster tails are classified as either warm water or cold water. The cold water tails are fished from South Africa to Australia and New Zealand. The warm water tails are landed from Florida to Brazil. Tails from South Africa are believed by many to have the best taste and texture, and have the highest price tag. In restaurants, the most popular seafood meal besides shrimp is the "surf & turf," consisting of a juicy tender cut steak and a lobster or lobster tail. Although lobster tails have a high retail value, usually above $20 per pound, they are comparable in value to live lobster on a pound-for-pound edible meat basis. A one-pound lobster may yield only ¼ pound of edible meat, most of which is found in the tail. Thus, a one-pound lobster on sale at $6.99 per pound actually costs $27.96 per pound for the meat you can eat.

Choosing a tail over a live lobster depends mostly on how you would like to present your meal and on your particular taste.

SPLITTING AND CLEANING LOBSTER

There are several popular methods of cooking lobster, and each is easy to do in the home. Live lobsters are mostly boiled or broiled. Boiling is as easy as placing the live lobster head first into a pot of boiling water and cooking it until the shells turn dark red. Broiling requires a bit more preparation. It is best to broil a split lobster or lobster tail. The technique is actually more of a butterfly, where both halves remain attached. This helps the meat cook more evenly. If you purchase live lobster and are planning to broil them, it is best to have the store where you purchase the lobster split it. Their knives are sharp, and doing it at home may provide some anxious moments for you or your children.

For those who insist on keeping the animal alive until just before cooking, splitting is simple to do. Chill the live lobster in the refrigerator to slow down its metabolism. Choose a long, wide butcher knife or Chinese cleaver. Place the live lobster on a cutting board with legs up and eyes facing toward you. Set the blade onto the center of the body lengthwise. Place a towel over the blade, and hit the blade with a mallet near the lobster's eyes. This action will kill the lobster as fast as possible. The legs will still move, but it is dead. Push the knife through the remainder of the body, down to the back of the shell, but do not cut through the back. Remove the knife, and with both hands, gently butterfly the lobster open, without separating the halves. Using a fork, remove the eyes, antennae and the tamale (greenish organ). Rinse the cavity and cook.

To split a tail, the method is the same but the tail is placed swimmer fins down on the board. Then the tail is split with one hit of the knife using a mallet. Once the shell is cracked, cut down through the meat, but not enough to separate the halves. Lobster tails are all meat, so there is no cleaning needed.

Once the lobster has been successfully split, it is ready to be broiled or stuffed and broiled. Because of their high water content, lobster and crab cook very fast. It is strongly suggested that you cook your side dishes first before cooking the lobster.

BASIC BOILED LOBSTER

  4 live lobsters (American or spiny)
  1 cup melted butter

Fill a large deep pot ¾ full with hot tap water and bring to a rolling boil. Place lobster in water, head down. (This will kill it quickly.) Cover the pot and boil for approximately 15 minutes. Melt butter in microwave. Remove lobster from water and serve hot with melted butter.

  To clean a whole lobster, once it has cooled enough to handle, split front segment with a knife and pull off antenna. Just inside the head there will be a sack of colored matter. This contains the internal organs of the animal. Using a fork, scrape out this section in one pull and remove the eyes as well. There is very little meat in the head or body area. Most of the meat is in the claws and tail.

SERVES 4.

SIDE DISH SUGGESTIONS: Baked potato and steamed asparagus or broccoli.

SPLIT AND BROILED LOBSTER (whole or tails)

  4 split lobsters or tails
  1 cup melted butter

Pre-heat the broiler. Place split lobster or tails on a broiler pan meat side down. Broil about 2 inches from heat for 3 minutes. Turn lobster meat-side up. Brush top lightly with melted butter. Broil for 5 to 7 minutes. Remove from heat and serve hot with melted butter.

Timing is the key: Broiling lobster perfectly requires practice. The best way to get this technique down is to use the fork test. When you remove a split lobster or lobster tail from the broiler, hold the end of the tail with a potholder, and insert a fork into the narrow meat end. Pull up on the meat gently. It will pull out of the shell easily and in one piece when cooked just right. If you have overcooked the meat, it will stick to the shell. This is your cue to reduce your cooking time on the next session. Your timing will improve each time you broil lobster. When broiling lobster, you need to stay at the oven and check them every other minute.

CLASSIC CRAB-STUFFED LOBSTER

4 split lobsters or tails
8 ounces blue crabmeat or snow crabmeat
¼ cup butter
¼ cup celery, finely chopped
¼ cup onion, finely chopped
1 egg
3 tablespoons mayonnaise
¼ teaspoon mustard
¼ teaspoon seafood seasoning
3 soda crackers, crushed

Melt butter in a skillet; add celery and onion and cook until soft. In a bowl, mix egg, mayonnaise, mustard, seafood seasoning, crabmeat, celery, onion, and cracker. Place crab stuffing in refrigerator to chill. Pre-heat the broiler. Place split lobster or tails on a broiler pan, meat side down. Broil about 2 inches from heat for 3 minutes. Turn lobster over. Place crab stuffing in the cavity of the lobster, or on top of the tail, and fold the butterfly tail partially to hold in place. Brush top of lobster with butter and return to broiler for 5 to 7 minutes. The mayonnaise in the stuffing will cause the top of the meat to brown. Watch carefully to avoid burning. When shells are red and stuffing is brown, remove from heat and serve.
SERVES 4.
SIDE DISH SUGGESTIONS: Salad and fresh sourdough bread.

LOBSTER THERMIDOR

4 lobster tails, 6 ounces or larger
2 tablespoons butter
2 tablespoons flour
1 teaspoon salt
2 tablespoons cooking sherry
½ teaspoon dry mustard
1 cup half-and-half
¼ teaspoon paprika
¼ teaspoon tarragon
¼ teaspoon chervil
2 egg yolks
½ cup heavy cream
2 drops Tabasco sauce

In a medium-sized pot, boil lobster tails until shells turn red (about 2 minutes). Remove from water even if slightly undercooked and chill under cold water immediately. Split tails and remove meat, arrange one tail per baking dish (using mini loaf pans or 1-pound loaf pans) and set aside. In a saucepan melt butter over low heat and mix with flour. Stirring constantly, add salt, sherry, mustard, half-and-half, paprika, tarragon, and chervil. Cook at medium-low heat until sauce is thickened. Add egg yolks, heavy cream, and Tabasco sauce. Stir over medium heat for 3 minutes, but do not allow sauce to boil. Pour Thermidor sauce over each lobster tail. Broil tails until tops turn golden brown.
SERVES 4.
SIDE DISH SUGGESTIONS: Fresh asparagus and boiled red-skinned potatoes.

See also:
Black Tie Affair Lobster-Caviar Dip, page 175
Lobster Chowder, page 141

OTHER SHELLFISH

SCALLOPS, CLAMS, OYSTERS, MUSSELS, CONCH, AND ABALONE

Shellfish are divided into two main groups known as crustaceans and mollusks. Crustaceans, which have an external skeleton and jointed legs, include shrimp, crabs, lobster, and crawfish. These are considered in other chapters.

The mollusk family is divided into three subgroups:
Bivalves (two-shelled): clams, oysters, mussels, and scallops.
Univalves (one-shelled): abalone and conch or snails.
Cephalopods: octopus, squid, and cuttlefish.

Molluscan shellfish family favorites

From Maine to Florida, east to west coast, oysters, scallops, clams, mussels, and conch have been traditional favorites for generations. Visitors to Cape Cod anxiously await the summer to enjoy beachside steamed or fried clams. What would any seafood restaurant be without a great clam chowder? Then there is grandma's recipe for Thanksgiving oyster stuffing. More oysters are sold during Thanksgiving week than any other time of the year, while in the southern Gulf states, no visit is complete until a tasty conch fritter has been enjoyed. Americans with European ancestry and visitors from other countries crave hot, steamy mussels from Maine. These traditions have made shellfish some of the most widely enjoyed seafoods in the world.

Each type of molluscan shellfish includes different species. The interesting thing about this entire family of seafood is that any species can be substituted in any recipe with equally enjoyable results. Most people want to purchase clams, mussels, and oysters alive to ensure the freshness of the shellfish. (Good, fresh bivalves close tight when they are alive. See the live shellfish buying chart, page 14, for more specifics.) Customers who desire oysters shucked (removed from shell) can buy them in 8-ounce and 16-ounce containers. The freshness is guaranteed by the "sell-by" date on the cans. It is illegal to sell any oysters beyond that date. Conch meat can usually be purchased frozen, cleaned raw, or cleaned cooked.

SCALLOPS

"Is it scallop or really punched-out shark meat?" This question has been asked for generations. Some fish processors may have used punched-out shark and skates in the past to create mock scallops. Yet, quite honestly, anyone who has ever tried to punch out round circles from shark meat or skate wings will tell you it is a time-consuming job. There is an easy way to tell if the scallops you buy are genuine. Unlike clams and oysters that sit on the bottom of the ocean, scallops swim. The swimming is accomplished by snapping the shell together and creating a jet of water to propel the animal through the water. This action develops a strong muscle that is attached to both shells and is used to open and close them. In the United States, it is only the white or cream-colored muscle, or "eye" as it is called, that is sent to market for consumption. When the scallop is shucked (cut from its shell), there is a small piece of elastic meat—the hinge of the muscle—which stays on the scallop meat. If you have any doubt as to the authenticity of the scallops on display, ask the seafood clerk to show it to you when you buy scallops. This is the true scallop trademark.

In other parts of the world, the scallop is shipped to the market alive. European and Asian cultures enjoy eating all parts of the animal.

Scallops get their name from the fluted edges of their colorful shells. There are three basic types of scallops: sea, bay, and calico. Taste, size, and availability of the catch determine the value of each on the retail market. Naturally, locals will claim that the type of scallops they harvest are the best.

Processors use a chemical called sodium tripolyphosphate (STP) to make seafood retain enough water during processing to prevent dehydration during freezing. Small amounts have a positive effect on certain species during processing. It is tempting to think that if a little is a good thing, then a lot must be better. In the case of STP nothing could be further from the truth. The scallop muscle has a natural ability to absorb an enormous amount of water. Too much STP causes a scallop to increase to several times its normal size. Customers can purchase what appears to be a very large scallop for its species type, only to find it shrinks to half its size when cooked. Excessive STP finds its way into scallops by "soaking": natural scallops are soaked in a tank of water with a large quantity of STP. Until recently, there was no federal regulation controlling the use of STP in scallops. Now the U.S. Government requires scallops with moisture above 80 percent to be labeled a "scallop product." Since this label is used only for wholesale and shipping purposes, however, wet-pack (soaked) and dry-pack scallops are sold in the market with no indication of the difference.

The best rule of thumb is: "you get what you pay for." True dry-pack scallops are always more expensive than wet-pack. The annual catch of scallops is low and declining. Therefore, you are unlikely to find dry-pack scallops at a low price.  When you see very large scallops, at an unbelievable price…don't believe it! These are most likely wet-pack.

A true dry scallop is somewhat flat in appearance. It has a high sugar content and when sautéed, it will caramelize. The meat will turn a dense white when cooked. A wet scallop tends to be abnormally round and plump and will stay translucent, even when over-cooked.

Sea scallops

The sea scallop is the largest of the three scallops, with a shell that measures up to 8 inches. Harvest takes place from Newfoundland to North Carolina. The New England coastal town of New Bedford in Massachusetts is famous for its centuries-old scallop-fishing fleets. Sea scallops are dredged in 180 to 600 feet of cold, deep Atlantic Ocean water. The fishing vessel uses a heavy chain link mesh net that is pulled along the ocean bottom where scallop beds are found. Sea scallops are sold by the pound, with the count per pound and type of pack (wet or dry) determining the range of price. Sea scallops have a unique taste all their own.

Bay scallops

These scallops are found along the coast of the New England and Mid-Atlantic states: Massachusetts, New York, Connecticut, Rhode Island, and New Jersey. Some are specific to a local region and carry a local name, such as the Long Island Bay scallop and the Peconic Bay scallop. Ask a seafood lover in Long Island where the best scallops come from and they will tell you, "Long Island." Fresh bay scallops from these areas seldom find their way outside the Mid-Atlantic/New England market. The bay scallop is smaller than the sea scallop, with a shell measuring 2 to 3 inches. If you are fortunate enough to live in an area where these scallops are sold, you will find them quite a delicacy.

Calico scallops

Currently the most concentrated fishing area for the calico scallop is off the coast of Florida in waters on both sides of the state. These scallops are very tiny; the muscle portion seldom exceeds the size of a kernel of popped popcorn. Calico scallops are the least expensive of all scallops. The flavor is sweet, yet not as rich as the sea or bay scallops. These small scallops work well in chowders and pasta. Harvest is unpredictable, with landings ranging from millions of pounds to zero.

Farm-raised scallops

The science of farm-raising scallops is relatively new. Initial success has been good and in a few years the product may reach marketable status. The growing period for farm-raised scallops is 22 months. China is currently shipping several million pounds of farm-raised bay scallops to the United States each year.

CLAMS

There are five basic types of clams: hard shell, soft shell, surf, razor, and geoduck. The harvest method is conducted in shallow waters using tongs, rakes, and mechanical suction. Harvest areas and sizing minimums are strictly regulated.

Clams are most abundant on the east coast of the United States. In the Pacific, the razor and geoduck (pronounced "goo-ee-duck") are most popular. The hard shell is marketed by size and known commercially in markets as littleneck, top neck, cherrystone, quahog, and chowder. The most popular for eating raw are the littleneck (the smaller and more expensive) and the cherrystone. Both are excellent for steaming. Ocean quahogs and surf clams are seldom sold unprocessed in the retail market.

These clams are the major ingredient used in the brand name chowders, stuffed clams, canned chopped clam meat, and clam juice commonly found on the grocery shelf.

Soft clams are a popular beach concession and ocean resort favorite. These are the clams that make the best fried clams, clams strips, and "belly clam," a New England favorite. Soft-shell clams have a recognizable protruding "foot," which is actually a siphon used to gather food.

How to shuck clams

Wash all clams thoroughly and discard dead ones. Let sit on ice for 15 minutes. Don't disturb.

Hold the clam in the palm of your hand and force the knife blade between the two shells.

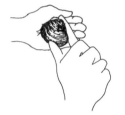

Run the knife around the edge of the clam to sever the muscles that hold the two shells closed.

Open the clam and discard the top shell. Loosen the meat from the shell and check for any shell fragments.

MUSSELS

Two types of mussels are marketed throughout the world, blue mussels and green mussels. Blue mussels are both farmed and harvested wild. Maine is the major producing state in the Atlantic area, and Washington is the Pacific mussel giant. Green mussels are mostly farmed in New Zealand, South America, and Africa.

Mussels are a lean meat food with many healthy attributes. For many years there was little demand for mussels in the United States beyond the producing areas, but Europeans have made mussels a regular part of their diet for centuries. Because of extensive marketing and a demand for more healthy foods, mussel consumption is growing rapidly worldwide. Mussels are truly one of the easiest seafood meals to prepare in the home.

OYSTERS

There are three basic types of oysters: Atlantic, Pacific, and European. The Atlantic and Pacific oysters are identified by the place of harvest, usually the name of an estuary (Apolachicola, Florida; Chincoteaque, Maryland; Ketchikan, Alaska). European oysters are mostly farm-raised in New England, California, Washington, France, and England with great success. Oysters are sold in the shell and fresh shucked by the ½ pint, pint, and gallon. The most common sizes are stewing, small, and select.

It was once believed that a rule of thumb for oyster consumption was that oysters could only be eaten in months with an "R." This popular rule no longer applies since modern-day refrigeration inhibits factors that caused concerns about eating oysters in the warmer months.

How to shuck oysters

Wash the oyster thoroughly and place it in the palm of your hand.

Force the knife between the shells. Pry the shell open by running the knife around the whole edge of the shell. This will cut the muscles that hold the two shells together.

Loosen the meat from the shell and check for any shell fragments.

Alternative method: insert a "church key" (old fashioned bottle opener) and pop off the top shell.

CONCH

These univalves are actually giant sea snails. Italians call them scungilli. In the Florida Keys they are simply conch. You may know these sea creatures best as the huge shells that you held up to your ear as a child to hear the sound of the ocean. Conch meat is described by some as being somewhat rubbery. A delicious conch fritter can change that opinion fast.

WHAT YOU NEED TO KNOW ABOUT RAW SHELLFISH

Stories involving the incidence of food poisoning naturally make the news. These stories may report a potential danger in eating seafood, while offering little solid information. Most instances of confirmed illness involve consumption of raw shellfish. Yet not all shellfish are a source of concern. Only a few species in the molluscan family— oysters, clams, and mussels—are a true cause for concern, because these animals are filter feeders.

A single mussel, clam, or oyster can filter up to 15 gallons of water per day in obtaining food. If water contamination or marine virus exists in the area where these animals feed, toxins may find their way into the human food supply. However, proper cooking effectively kills bacteria or viruses. Many consumers do eat raw shellfish without becoming ill, but a risk definitely exists.

People in coastal states eat a great deal of raw fish. The incidence of illness is quite low, however, because molluscan shellfish harvest is regulated under the state-by-state mandated National Shellfish Sanitation Program (NSSP). Each day, the state marine agency responsible for the program monitors water conditions in oyster, clam, and mussel beds. When water conditions are found to be unacceptable for harvest due to storm runoff or red tide (a naturally occurring marine algae bloom), the beds in those areas are posted closed. The system has been shown to be highly effective in keeping contaminated shellfish off the market. (For more information, see **Basic Seafood Facts,** on page 4.)

Oyster   Mussel   Clam

BROILED SCALLOPS

1 pound fresh or frozen scallops (any type)
vegetable oil spray
3 tablespoons melted butter (or use vegetable oil spray)
1 tablespoon lemon-pepper seasoning
1 tablespoon fresh parsley, chopped

Pre-heat the broiler. Use fingers or a knife to pull off the hinge strap. (Frozen scallops should be thawed in refrigerator overnight prior to cooking.) Spray the broiler tray with vegetable oil spray. Place scallops on tray, drizzle with melted butter, and sprinkle with lemon-pepper seasoning and fresh chopped parsley. Broil about 2 inches from heat. Cook until scallops turn white and tops are lightly browned (about 5 minutes). Remove from heat and serve hot.

SERVES 3.

SIDE DISH SUGGESTIONS: Red potato salad and freshly baked bread sticks.

"FRY 'EM UP" BOSTON-STYLE SCALLOPS

1 pound scallops (any type)
1 egg
¼ cup milk
1 cup flour
¼ teaspoon salt
¼ teaspoon pepper
1 cup bread crumbs
2 cups vegetable oil

Use fingers or a knife to pull off hinge straps. (Frozen scallops should be thawed in refrigerator overnight prior to cooking.) Beat egg and milk in a deep bowl. Add scallops to bowl and let stand for 5 minutes. Remove scallops from bowl and dredge in flour, rolling them gently to coat evenly. Salt and pepper the scallops. Using fingers or a fork, dip scallops back into egg and milk; roll in bread crumbs. Set aside on plate until all scallops have been breaded. Add oil to deep skillet or pot and place on high heat. When oil is bubbling slightly, place scallops in pan and fry until golden brown. Cooking time is about 3 minutes. Remove from oil, and place on paper towel to drain. Serve scallops hot.

SERVES 3.

SIDE DISH SUGGESTIONS: French fries and coleslaw.

EASY SAUTÉ SCALLOPS LIGHTLY SEASONED

1 pound scallops (any type)
1 tablespoon seafood seasoning (Chef Paul Prudhomme's
    blackened Redfish Magic or any Cajun seasoning)
3 tablespoons butter (or use vegetable oil spray)

Use fingers or a knife to pull off hinge straps. (Frozen scallops should be thawed in refrigerator overnight prior to cooking.) Select a medium-sized skillet and spray with vegetable oil spray or add butter. Turn heat to medium/high and add scallops evenly around surface of the skillet. Allow one side to cook for 2 minutes. Then turn each scallop and lightly sprinkle tops with seasoning. Cook for 3 minutes. Using a spatula, gently turn the scallops several times to allow the seasoning to get into the entire scallop. Remove scallops from heat and serve hot. (Allow 1 to 1½ minutes more cooking time for very large scallops.)
SERVES 3.
SIDE DISH SUGGESTIONS: Toasted French bread and white shoe peg corn.

LISBON SCALLOPS AND BROCCOLI

1 pound sea or bay scallops
1 bunch fresh broccoli
½ cup butter
1 clove garlic, finely chopped
½ bunch fresh parsley, finely chopped
½ teaspoon salt
1 teaspoon pepper
½ teaspoon lemon juice

Fill a pot ¾ full of hot tap water and bring to a boil. Cut broccoli into florets. Blanch broccoli in boiling water until it turns vivid green (about 2 minutes). Drain broccoli and set aside. Melt butter in a medium-sized deep skillet at medium heat. Add garlic and parsley to hot butter. Stir until garlic is toasted. Add scallops (if sea scallops are being used, slice them in half). Stir-fry scallops until they turn white, about 4 minutes. Add broccoli, salt, pepper, and lemon juice. Reduce heat to low and let sauté for 2 minutes.
SERVES 3 to 4.
SIDE DISH SUGGESTIONS: Mashed potatoes or freshly baked bread.

SCALLOP MUSHROOM NEWBURG

1 pound sea or bay scallops
3 tablespoons butter
4 large fresh mushrooms, finely chopped
1 tablespoon flour
1 cup cream
½ teaspoon salt
½ teaspoon nutmeg
1 tablespoon cooking sherry
1 egg yolk
French bread, unsliced

Melt butter in a skillet. Sauté scallops and mushrooms at medium heat until scallops turn white. Mix flour, cream, salt, nutmeg, sherry, and egg yolk. Pour over mushrooms and scallops. Reduce heat to low, stir until sauce thickens, and simmer for 5 minutes. Serve over broiler-toasted French bread slices.

Broiler-toasted French bread: Pre-heat broiler. Slice bread at an angle. Melt butter in microwave. Brush both sides of bread with butter. Sprinkle with Romano cheese if desired. Place on broiler tray and allow top to brown. Turn and toast opposite side.

SERVES 3 to 4.

SIDE DISH SUGGESTIONS: Tossed salad and applesauce.

COQUILLES SAINT JACQUES

1½ pounds scallops (bay or sea, fresh or frozen)
vegetable spray
¾ cup butter, melted
2 cloves garlic, chopped fine
½ cup bread crumbs, unflavored
salt and pepper to taste
½ cup buttery type crackers, crushed coarse
1 tablespoon fresh parsley, chopped

Note: Thaw scallops if using frozen. Remove hinge straps if using sea scallops.

Preheat the oven to 350 degrees F. For individual servings, select 4 ramekins, or a 9x9-inch baking dish for family style. Spray with light coating of vegetable spray. Melt butter with garlic in microwave for 30–40 seconds. Sprinkle dish with a light dusting of bread crumbs with salt and pepper. Add scallops and sprinkle crushed crackers over each. Drizzle melted garlic butter over each scallop. Garnish top with fresh chopped parsley. Bake for 15 minutes. Switch the oven to broil and toast top about two inches from heat.

SERVES: 2 to 4.

SIDE DISH SUGGESTIONS: French style string beans and wild rice.

BACK BAY CLAM FRITTERS

1 pound fresh or canned chopped clams
1 small onion, finely chopped
1 sweet red pepper, finely chopped
2 stalks celery, finely chopped
2 tablespoons butter
1 egg
¼ cup milk
¼ cup cornmeal
¼ cup pancake mix
1 teaspoon baking powder
¼ teaspoon red pepper
2 cups vegetable oil

Add onion, sweet pepper, and celery to a small skillet with clams and butter. Cook for 5 minutes at medium heat. In a large mixing bowl, combine egg, milk, cornmeal, pancake mix, baking powder, and red pepper. Add cooked ingredients and mix. Place oil in a deep pot, allow to bubble at high heat; then place tablespoon-sized portions of fritter mix into hot oil. Cook only until golden. Remove fritter and drain on paper towel. All of the ingredients in the fritter mix are fully cooked; you only need to brown the batter to make it firm.

SERVES 6 to 8.

Farm-raised
Florida
littleneck clam

STEAMED CLAMS IN GARLIC BUTTER

    2 dozen live littleneck clams OR
        2 pounds live soft-shell steamer clams
    2 cups water or beer
    4 cloves garlic, finely chopped
    1 onion, finely chopped
    4 tablespoons butter

Rinse clams in cold running water and brush away any sand on shells. In a large soup stockpot, add water or beer, garlic, onion, and butter. Place pot on medium/high heat, bring to a boil, and add clams. Cover pot and allow 6 minutes cooking time. Remove lid and inspect clams. Clams will open wide and the meat will shrink away from the shells when done. Serve clams hot. Pour cooking juices in a bowl to use as dipping sauce.

Variation: Replace butter and water with a marinara sauce. Serve over angel hair pasta.

SERVES 4 to 6.

SIDE DISH SUGGESTIONS: The perfect cookout appetizer with hot dogs or hamburgers.

CLAMS OREGANO

    2 dozen live littleneck clams
    1 egg
    2 cloves garlic, finely chopped
    ¼ cup fresh parsley, finely chopped
    6 tablespoons oregano
    2½ cups bread crumbs
    3 tablespoons olive oil
    1 cup shredded mozzarella

Scrub clams under cold running water to remove sand. Open clams with a clam knife if experienced. Otherwise place clams in a brown paper bag and microwave at high heat for 1 minute. Open bag and check each clam. Shell should be slightly popped open, but the meat will still be raw. Split shells with knife, allowing meat to remain in one half. Pre-heat the oven to 425 degrees F. Mix egg, garlic, parsley, oregano, bread crumbs, and olive oil. Stuff each clam with equal amounts of stuffing. Sprinkle tops with cheese and bake for 10 minutes.

SERVES 6 to 8.

CLAMS CASINO

2 dozen littleneck or cherrystone clams
3 cups rock salt
5 slices bacon
¼ cup butter
1 green pepper, finely chopped
5 pimentos, chopped
½ bunch fresh parsley, finely chopped
2 tablespoons hot sauce

Pre-heat the broiler. Layer rock salt in a baking pan or deep cookie sheet. Scrub clams in cold running water to remove sand. Open clams with a clam knife if experienced. Otherwise, place clams in a brown paper bag and microwave at high heat for 1 minute. Each shell should be slightly popped open, but the meat will still be raw. Use a butter knife to separate shells and leave meat in one shell. Microwave bacon until nearly crisp. Chop bacon and add to butter in a small saucepan with green pepper, pimento, and parsley. Sauté until pepper is soft. Spoon stuffing onto each clam. Place clams on rock salt bed. Add one dash of hot sauce and broil for 12 minutes, 2 inches from heat.
SERVES 4 to 6.

EASY CLAMS AND LINGUINI WITH RED SAUCE

24 littleneck or pasta clams
1 green bell pepper, finely chopped
1 clove fresh garlic, finely chopped
1 small onion, finely chopped
1 15-ounce can tomato sauce
1 6-ounce tomato paste
¼ cup cooking sherry
1 teaspoon salt
1 tablespoon olive oil
1 pound linguini

In a 2-quart pot, combine vegetables, tomato sauce, tomato paste, sherry, salt and oil. Cover pot and cook slow on medium/low heat for 40 minutes. After 30 minutes, cook linguini according to instructions on package. During last 10 minutes of cooking sauce, add washed clams. Stir all clams into hot sauce. Drain and rinse pasta under cold water. Place portions on serving dishes, topping each serving with sauce and 4 to 6 clams.
SERVES: 4 to 6.
SIDE DISH SUGGESTIONS: Tossed garden salad and imported cheeses.

CLAMS ROCKEFELLER

2 dozen live littleneck clams
5 strips of bacon
2 stalks of celery, finely chopped
1 medium onion, finely chopped
2 tablespoons fresh parsley, finely chopped
4 tablespoons butter
1 tablespoon anisette
5 ounces frozen chopped spinach, thawed and drained
3 tablespoons flavored bread crumbs

Scrub clams in cold running water to remove sand. Open clams with a clam knife if experienced. Otherwise, place clams in a brown paper bag and microwave at high heat for 1 minute. Open bag and check each clam. Shell should be slightly popped open, but the meat will still be raw. Use a butter knife to separate shells and leave meat in one of the shells. Pre-heat the oven to 450 degrees F. Microwave bacon until nearly crisp. Remove from microwave and cut into thirds. Add celery, onion, and parsley to skillet and sauté in skillet with butter at medium heat until vegetables are soft. Add bread crumbs, anisette, and spinach and then remove from heat. Stuff each clam with equal amounts of stuffing. Place one piece of bacon over top and bake for 10 to 15 minutes.
SERVES 6 to 8.

LONG ISLAND FRIED CLAM STRIPS

24 cherrystone clams, surf clams, or canned clams
½ cup flour
½ cup cornmeal
2 cups vegetable oil
2 eggs
½ cup milk
1 teaspoon salt
½ teaspoon black pepper

Scrub clams in cold running water to remove sand. Open clams with a clam knife if experienced. Otherwise, place clams in a brown paper bag and microwave at high heat for 1 minute. Open bag and check each clam. Shell should be slightly popped open, but the meat will still be raw. Use a paring knife to separate shells and remove meat. Cut each clam in half, ¾ of the way through. Pre-heat oil in a deep pot at medium/high heat.

Mix eggs, milk, salt, and pepper in a bowl, and then add clams. Combine flour and cornmeal in a Ziploc bag. Drop each clam into bag, seal bag, and shake to coat. Fry clams until golden. Drain on a paper towel to remove excess oil.

SERVES 4 to 6.

SIDE DISH SUGGESTION: Sliced carrots and celery in cucumber sauce. (Mix one pureed cucumber with 2 cups sour cream, ½ cup heavy cream, 2 tablespoons dill, and 1 teaspoon lemon juice.)

See also:
Clam and Pimento Dip, page 173
Manhattan Clam Chowder, page 141
New England Clam Chowder, page 142

OYSTERS ROCKEFELLER

    2 dozen live oysters in the shell
    5 strips of bacon
    2 stalks of celery, finely chopped
    1 medium onion, finely chopped
    2 tablespoons fresh parsley, finely chopped
    4 tablespoons butter
    3 tablespoons flavored bread crumbs
    1 tablespoon anisette
    5 ounces frozen chopped spinach, thawed and drained

Scrub oysters in cold running water to remove sand. Shuck oysters if you have experience. Otherwise, use the microwave to cook until oysters open. Place oysters in a brown paper bag in microwave at high heat for 1 minute. Check each oyster. Shells should be slightly popped open, but the meat will still be raw. Microwave any oysters again that did not open.

Use a knife to separate shells and allow meat to remain in the deeper of the two shells. Pre-heat the oven to 450 degrees F. Microwave bacon until nearly crisp. Remove from microwave and cut into thirds. Add celery, onion, and parsley to skillet and sauté with butter at medium heat until vegetables are soft. Add anisette, spinach, and bread crumbs; remove from heat. Cover each oyster with a layer of vegetable mixture. Place one piece of bacon over top and bake for 10 to 15 minutes.

SERVES: 6 to 8.

SIDE DISH SUGGESTION: Tortilla chips and salsa.

DEEP-FRIED OYSTERS IN CRACKER MEAL

2 pints shucked, raw oysters, any size
1 egg
¼ cup milk
½ teaspoon salt
½ teaspoon pepper
¼ teaspoon hot sauce
2 cups vegetable oil
2 cups cracker meal

Drain and rinse oysters under cold water. Pre-heat oil in 2-quart pan at medium/high heat. Mix egg, milk, salt, pepper, and hot sauce in a bowl. Pour cracker meal onto a sheet of wax paper. Dip oysters in the egg/milk mixture and then, one at a time, into the cracker meal, patting gently to cover well. Once all oysters are breaded, immediately drop them into the hot oil. Fry until cracker meal browns. Pay close attention to the cooking—cracker meal browns quickly and burns if not removed from the heat in time. Place oysters on a paper towel to drain excess oil.

SERVES 4 to 6.

SIDE DISH SUGGESTIONS: Coleslaw and rice pilaf.

GRANDMA'S AUTHENTIC THANKSGIVING OYSTER STUFFING

1 pint raw, shucked oysters, any size
1 loaf bread
2 tablespoons butter
2 stalks celery, finely chopped
1 small onion, finely chopped
1 egg
½ teaspoon poultry seasoning
¼ teaspoon salt
½ teaspoon pepper

Break bread into small pieces in a bowl. Chop drained oysters into fine pieces. In a skillet add butter, celery, onion, and oysters and cook on medium until soft. Mix in egg. Add mixture to bread and mix with hands. If stuffing is too dry, add juice from oysters or a small amount of water.

Option: Add sautéed oysters, onion, and celery to any pre-mixed prepared stuffing.

SERVES 6 to 8.

See also: **Oyster Stew,** page 142

KEY WEST-STYLE CONCH FRITTERS

1 pound cooked, peeled conch, finely chopped
1 small onion, finely chopped
1 red bell pepper, finely chopped
2 stalks celery, finely chopped
2 tablespoons butter
1 egg
¼ cup milk
¼ cup cornmeal
¼ cup pancake mix
1 teaspoon baking powder
¼ teaspoon red pepper
2 cups vegetable oil

Horseradish dipping sauce:
2 tablespoons mayonnaise
¼ teaspoon horseradish
1 squeeze of lemon juice

Place conch meat, onion, sweet pepper, and celery in small skillet with butter on medium heat and cook until vegetables are soft. In a large mixing bowl, combine egg, milk, cornmeal, pancake mix, baking powder, and red pepper. Add cooked ingredients and mix. Pour oil into a deep pot, allow to bubble at high heat. Place tablespoon-sized portions of fritter mix into hot oil. Cook only until golden. Remove fritters and drain on paper towel. Since all the fritter mix ingredients are already fully cooked, you only need to brown the batter enough to make it firm. Mix ingredients for horseradish dipping sauce and serve on side. SERVES 4 to 6.

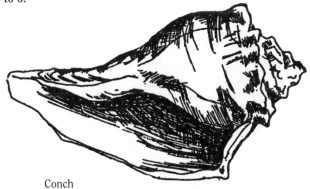

Conch

SWEET MUSSELS FROM MAINE

4 pounds live mussels
2 green bell peppers, finely chopped
1 red onion, finely chopped
3 cloves garlic, finely chopped
1 bunch fresh scallions, finely chopped
2 cups water or cooking sherry
3 tablespoons butter

Rinse mussels in cold running water. Pull off any beards (silky, thread-like material) that may be on the shells. In a large soup stockpot, combine chopped peppers, onion, garlic, scallions, water or sherry, and butter. Place pot on medium/high heat and bring to a boil. Add mussels, cover, and cook for 5 to 7 minutes. Remove lid; mussels will be open when done. Serve hot, with pot juices poured over the mussels.

SERVES 2 to 4.

SIDE DISH SUGGESTIONS: Crusty French or Italian bread.

See also: **Belgian Mussel Salad**, page 150

FRIED ABALONE MEDALLIONS

1 pound fresh abalone meat
2 cups vegetable oil
1 egg
¼ cup milk
1 teaspoon garlic, chopped
½ cup flour
2 cups ground butter crackers
1 teaspoon salt

Slice abalone into 2-inch medallions. Pre-heat oil in 2-quart saucepan at medium/high heat. Mix egg, milk, and garlic in a bowl. Place medallions in liquid. Mix flour, ground crackers, and salt, and spread over sheet of wax paper. Dredge each medallion in breading, and place in oil. Fry until golden brown. Remove from oil and place on paper towel to drain excess oil.

SERVES 2 to 4.

SIDE DISH SUGGESTIONS: Macaroni salad and Greek olives.

V

SALMON

THE MOST POPULAR FISH IN THE WORLD

Salmon is rich in omega-3 acids and is one of the best tasting fish in the world. In terms of global consumption and acceptance, salmon is second only to shrimp. More than 15 countries farm-raise salmon, and that is just one segment of the salmon industry. The wild catch in the Pacific Northwest is just as significant. Although the wild salmon "run" has occurred for thousands of years, the first recorded commercial fishery in western North America began in the early 1800s when the first salmon was salted and shipped to the eastern United States. Salmon has been widely marketed since the seventeenth century in Scotland and most of Europe. Today, "jet fresh" salmon arrives daily, to every continent in the world.

Salmon is not one single species of fish, but rather several species. The most common globally farm-raised salmon is the Atlantic salmon (*Salmo salar*). You will see this species year round in your supermarket or fish store more commonly than any other salmon. Although the name of this species is "Atlantic salmon," the fish is farmed in Chile, Norway, Scotland, the Pacific Northwest, and eastern Canada and comes from different oceans. Countries that produce Atlantic salmon often try to gain name recognition by adding the regional name: for example, Norwegian salmon, Chilean salmon, and Scottish smoked salmon are all Atlantic salmon. Currently, the major supplier of

Atlantic farm-raised salmon is Chile. Coastal conditions and water temperatures in Chile offer a good natural growing environment.

There are six species of salmon that are predominantly found in the Pacific Northwest and are mostly wild harvest. Each has a common name and a market name:

Common Name	Market Name
Coho salmon	Silver
King salmon	Chinook
Chum salmon	Keta
Pink salmon	Humpback
Sockeye salmon	Red, blueback
Cherry salmon	Cherry

Salmon recipes seldom suggest any particular species of salmon, although the taste and texture may vary from one type to another. It can be difficult to tell one species from another, because you will seldom see the whole salmon in its natural state. Fresh salmon fillets and steaks are commonly found in the marketplace, and to the untrained eye the species can look alike.

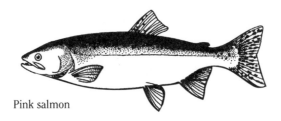

Pink salmon

Since wild salmon production enters the marketplace for a short period during the summer months, you can expect to see less Atlantic salmon during this time. On the west coast of the United States, customers have the opportunity to see more of the wild catch in whole and processed forms. Consumers who are close to the wild harvest region seem to prefer wild salmon to farm raised.

The Atlantic, the king or Chinook, the coho, and chum are the major commercial salmon in the European and North American markets for fresh and smoked salmon. Sockeye and pink salmon are sold mostly canned. The cherry salmon is harvested from South Korea to Japan, with Japan using most of the production.

DIFFERENCES AMONG SPECIES

Atlantic salmon
Milder in flavor than wild salmon, it has soft texture, with a nice flakiness when cooked. The color of the meat is deep pink to rich orange. The meat is oily and rich in omega-3 fatty acids, yet less fatty than the Chinook or king.

King salmon
Characterized by rich buttery flavor, a soft texture, and red meat, king is the largest in size of all the salmon. It is high in fatty content, and rich in omega-3s.

Chum salmon
Chum has a mild flavor due to its lower fatty content. The color is pink to light orange, even sometimes pale in comparison with other salmon species. Chums offer less omega-3 benefits than other salmon.

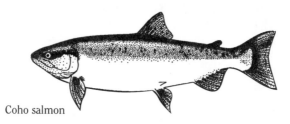

Coho salmon

Coho salmon
This is a small fish with good farming production in addition to wild runs. It is sold whole in some markets in the summer. Coho has a mild flavor and is an excellent fish to grill whole. The color of the flesh is semi-red to orange. Cohos are high in omega-3s.

Sockeye salmon
Sockeye is rich in flavor due to its high fatty content. The firm texture makes this a good grilling fish. A large quantity of the annual production is canned and often referred to as "red salmon." Sockeyes are very rich in omega-3s.

Note: Any fresh salmon available in your market can be successfully used in the salmon recipes in this chapter.

THE PACIFIC NORTHWEST SALMON RUN

A very large portion of the Pacific salmon fishery is structured around the annual wild salmon "run." Every year, wild salmon return to the stream in which they were born. It is the only place they will spawn. Different species return at different periods of their life cycles. Some may return after two years, others after four or five. Sooner or later they will all literally swim or "run" upstream to return to that natal river. Some salmon have been known to swim 2,000 miles or more during the spawning season. Modern run management uses statistical data to determine a reasonable projection of how many fish of each species type will return to its natal stream each year. This information allows producing states fairly accurate information to control the annual harvest and ensure that this amazing resource will be sustained.

BROILED SALMON A LA RITZ

   2 6– to 8–ounce portions fresh salmon fillet, skin on
   vegetable oil spray
   4 tablespoons melted butter
   ½ cup Ritz crackers, crushed
   ¼ teaspoon salt
   ¼ teaspoons pepper

Pre-heat the broiler. Spray broiler tray with vegetable oil. Place salmon on broiler tray, skin side down. Broil for 5 minutes. Brush melted butter over fillet. Sprinkle crushed crackers, salt, and pepper on top of fish. Broil for 5 minutes. Check center of salmon by flaking it with a fork to see if meat is cooked. Although salmon is pink in color, when cooked it turns whitish. If the center is still dark pink and translucent, return to broiler for 2 more minutes. Remove from heat and serve hot.
SERVES 2.
SIDE DISH SUGGESTIONS: Long grain wild rice and spinach.

BAKED SALMON WITH LEMON-CAPER SAUCE

   1½ pounds salmon fillets, skin on
   vegetable spray
   2 tablespoons butter
   2 tablespoons flour
   1 cup whole milk

1 teaspoon lemon juice
1 tablespoon capers
1 tablespoon fresh parsley, chopped
salt and pepper to taste

Pre-heat the oven to 375 degrees F. Spray a baking tray or dish with vegetable spray. Check salmon fillets for pin bones along center of fish and remove with tweezers if found. Place salmon on tray or dish skin side down. Bake for 15 minutes. While fish is baking, melt butter in a small saucepan at low heat. Stir in flour and cook until bubbly. Slowly add milk, lemon juice, capers, and chopped parsley, stirring constantly until thickened. Bring to a bubble, remove from heat, and set aside. Check fish by flaking center with a fork. Salmon perfectly cooked should be pinkish white throughout, yet moist. Place fish on serving dishes and spoon on sauce. Sprinkle with salt and pepper to taste. SERVES 2 to 4.

SIDE DISH SUGGESTIONS: Boiled carrots and rice pilaf.

GRILLED SALMON STEAKS

1 pound salmon steaks, ¾ inch thick
½ cup fresh parsley, chopped
¼ cup soy sauce
1 tablespoon lemon juice
1 teaspoon mayonnaise
½ teaspoon coarse black pepper
vegetable spray

Pre-heat the grill. Mix parsley, soy sauce, lemon juice, mayonnaise, and pepper to make a marinade/basting liquid. Spray grill with vegetable oil. Dip salmon steaks in liquid. Place salmon steaks on grill for one minute. Then turn to sear both sides quickly. Baste tops of steaks with liquid. Cook for 10 minutes. Baste as often as needed. Remove one steak from heat and flake the center to see if it is done to your satisfaction. Center should be opaque and very light in color. Return to grill if more cooking is needed. Otherwise, remove fish from grill and serve hot. SERVES 2 to 3.

SIDE DISH SUGGESTIONS: Yellow rice and black beans.

BAKED STUFFED SALMON

1 pound fresh salmon fillets, skin on
1 10-ounce can cream of mushroom soup
½ cup bread crumbs
vegetable spray
2 ounces New York sharp cheddar cheese

Pre-heat oven to 425 degrees F. Mix cream of mushroom soup and bread crumbs to a meatball-type consistency. Add more bread crumbs if needed. Place salmon fillets on a cutting board, skin side down. Use a sharp knife to cut a wide V shape down the center of the length of the salmon fillets. Do not cut through the skin. Pull the V strip of meat back, remove, and set aside. This will create a cavity for stuffing. Spray baking dish with vegetable oil and place fillet in dish skin side down. Switch oven to broil and cook fillets for 2 minutes, approximately 2 inches from heat. Remove baking dish from heat. Switch oven to bake, put soup and breadcrumb stuffing gently into the V cut and also spread over top of fish. Place previously removed strip of fish over the top of stuffing. Return to oven and bake for 12 minutes. Place slices of sharp cheese over stuffing and bake until cheese melts. Remove from oven and serve hot.

SERVES 3.

SIDE DISH SUGGESTIONS: Fresh steamed broccoli, white rice and carrots.

CLASSIC POACHED SALMON

1 pound salmon fillets, skin on (pin bones removed)

Poaching fumet (liquid):
½ cup scallions, coarsely chopped
1 celery stalk, coarsely chopped
1 carrot, coarsely chopped
1 bunch parsley, coarsely chopped
4 cups water
1 teaspoon salt
2 tablespoon lemon juice
1 teaspoon dill weed

To make fumet: Chop scallions, celery, carrot, and parsley. Fill pot with 4 cups of water, and add chopped vegetables, lemon juice, salt, and dill. Bring to a boil. Cover pot and cook for 15 minutes on low heat.

To poach: Wrap salmon fillets in a cheesecloth and twist both ends. Uncover fumet and gently lower the wrapped fish into the liquid, allowing ends of cloth to rest slightly over lip of pot, but far enough from heat to avoid fire. Increase heat to medium and wait until liquid begins to bubble, then time the cooking to about 10 minutes. Remove fish; carefully unwrap onto serving dish. Cut into serving sizes and enjoy hot or cold.

SERVES 2 to 3.

SIDE DISH SUGGESTIONS: Steamed cauliflower and candied yams.

GRANNY'S OLD-FASHIONED SALMON CAKES

    1 pound salmon fillets
    2 cups water
    2 slices dry bread
    ½ bunch fresh parsley, finely chopped
    ¼ cup onion, finely chopped
    ¼ teaspoon salt
    ¼ teaspoon pepper
    1 egg
    2 tablespoons mayonnaise
    2 cups flour
    ½ cup vegetable oil

Place salmon fillets on cutting board. Run fingers carefully along fillet and feel for bones. (The term "fillet" does not mean "boneless." Some fillets have few to no bones, but there is no guarantee.) Remove any bones with tweezers or knife. In a large pot bring 2 cups water to a boil. Place a colander in pot and layer fish along sides. Steam fish until it turns white. Remove from heat, allow cooling, and flake into pieces in a large mixing bowl. Crumble dry bread over salmon and sprinkle with parsley, onion, salt, and pepper. In a small bowl whisk egg and mayonnaise; pour over salmon. Mix gently with hands and shape into tight, flat 2-inch cakes. Place flour on a large sheet of waxed paper, and roll each salmon cake into flour. Add oil to skillet, place on medium heat and fry cakes until golden, turning as needed.

SERVES 3 to 4.

SIDE DISH SUGGESTIONS: Crackers and fresh sliced garden vegetables.

SPECTACULAR SALMON LOAF

1 pound fresh salmon fillets, skinless, boneless
1 medium onion, finely chopped
½ teaspoon salt
½ teaspoon pepper
1 egg
1 6-ounce can tomato paste
¾ cup unflavored bread crumbs
1 cup ketchup
vegetable spray
1 fresh lemon, thinly sliced
1 tablespoon fresh dill, chopped

Pre-heat the oven to 350 degrees F. Use a sharp knife to chop salmon fillets into coarse pieces. In a large mixing bowl combine salmon, onion, salt, pepper, egg, tomato paste, and bread crumbs. Spray a 3x5 inch loaf pan with vegetable spray. Form salmon mixture into a loaf. Cover top of loaf with ketchup, sliced lemon and dill. Bake for 30 minutes. To remove loaf from dish, turn baking dish onto one plate and allow loaf to drop out. Then place another plate over bottom of loaf, place hands on both sides of plates and turn loaf rightside up. SERVES 4 to 6.

SIDE DISH SUGGESTIONS: Chopped spinach and mashed potatoes.

See also:

Smoked Salmon Party Dip, page 174
Smoked Salmon Logs with Hazelnuts, page 172
Chapter 17, Fun with Sushi

TUNA

GREAT TUNA WITHOUT THE CAN

Want to know just how enormous the tuna fishery is? Take a map of the world and draw a straight line from the bottom end of Chile across to New Zealand. Now draw another line from the top of Washington state east to the top of Japan. Color everything in between these lines and you have the free roaming area of tuna. There are only two other popular fish that span the globe as well: mahi-mahi and swordfish. All of these fish are fast-swimming, highly migratory marine animals that range far into the open sea. The largest tuna, the bluefin, can weigh an average of 1,500 pounds and measure over 10 feet in length.

Tuna species are the most consumed fish in the United States. Canned tuna, because of its low cost and ease of preparation, accounts for the lion's share of that consumption. Fresh tuna captures only a small fraction of the total. Many people have never tried fresh tuna. They know tuna simply as a salad with mayonnaise and celery on bread or a bun. Perhaps one of the best-kept secrets in the fish business is that fresh tuna on the grill is outstanding. Those who eat fresh tuna often, when asked what it tastes like, will say that it has a texture like that of beefsteak. Indeed, fresh tuna does have a rich taste and a firm, steak-like texture. When cooked, it provides large, delicious flakes of meat.

HARVEST

There are four main species of tuna: albacore, bluefin, yellowfin and skipjack. For centuries, the method for catching the fast-swimming tuna was hook and line. Midway through the twentieth century, purse-seine nets began to be used more frequently. Today, concerns over dolphin kills in tuna-rich fishing regions has had major impact on the tuna-fishing industry. Of the four major species of tuna, the dolphins tend to be close swimmers with yellowfin and skipjack tuna. Most of the concern about dolphin safety is focused on tuna fishing in the eastern tropical Pacific.

A QUICK LOOK AT THE DIFFERENT TUNA

Albacore
This species is considered by many consumers to be the premium white meat tuna. By law, it is the only one allowed to be labeled "white meat." Fresh-cooked albacore is rich in taste.

Bluefin
Due to its high fat content, it is regarded as the most desirable tuna for sushi. The very best bluefin gets the highest mark of number one *sashimi* grade, meaning it is the best tuna consumed raw. The best bluefin tuna is rushed to Japan, where it commands top prices in the marketplace. Sashimi, which consists of very thin slices of raw fish, is served in Japanese and Korean sushi bars. Bluefin is rich in omega-3s.

Yellowfin
The largest portion of the harvest is canned. U.S. consumers eat this species more than any other tuna, both as canned and fresh. You will see this product most often labeled "chunk light" canned tuna. It is rich in omega-3s.

Bluefin tuna

Skipjack

This tuna fits the "light meat" category, yet seldom finds its way to the market sold fresh. Sport fishermen enjoy catching skipjack and a similar-looking close relative, the bonita.

SAFETY NOTE

Raw tuna, along with mackerel, mahi-mahi, and bluefish, **must be kept cold—under 40 degrees.** At higher temperatures it produces the toxin histamine. People with respiratory challenges can react to high histamine levels and develop difficulty breathing. (Seafood processors, retailers, and restaurants are aware of these safety concerns and strive to keep seafood at proper temperatures.) When purchasing raw fish, it is advisable to return home and refrigerate it immediately. If this is not possible, ask the retailer to give you a bag of ice and pack the fish in a portable cooler.

GRILLED TUNA WITH FAR EAST MARINADE

1½ pounds tuna steaks (2 portions, ¾ inch thick)

Marinade

2 small yellow onions, finely chopped
4 large mushrooms, finely chopped
1 tablespoon soy sauce
1 teaspoon sugar
1 tablespoon cornstarch
2 tablespoons water
vegetable oil spray

Pre-heat the grill. Combine onions and mushrooms in a small saucepan with soy sauce and sugar. Bring to a boil, then reduce heat. Mix cornstarch in a cup with water and stir until creamy; add to saucepan and stir until thickened. Remove from heat and pour into a shallow bowl. Place tuna steaks in marinade for 5 minutes. Spray grill with vegetable oil. Place tuna on grill for 1 minute to sear, then turn. Baste top of steaks with marinade and continue to cook for 10 minutes. Check center of steak by using a fork to flake the meat. Tuna continues to cook even when removed from heat, so when center is just a bit translucent, it can be removed from heat and allowed to finish cooking on the serving plate.

SERVES 2 to 3.

SIDE DISH SUGGESTION: Steamed pea pods and pasta salad.

PERFECT BAKED TUNA

1 pound fresh tuna steak (2 portions, ¾ inch thick)
1 tablespoon margarine
½ teaspoon salt
¼ teaspoon pepper
¼ teaspoon lemon juice

The secret to perfect tuna is to avoid overcooking. Tuna is very moist and has a high oil content, but when overcooked it becomes very dry and lacks flavor. You must actually undercook it slightly to prepare perfect tuna. Cooking tuna requires strict attention and is more a matter of visual monitoring than actual cooking time. The more you cook tuna, the more expert you will become in judging when it is perfectly done.

Pre-heat oven to 425 degrees F. Coat the bottom of a glass baking dish with margarine. Place tuna steaks into dish and sprinkle each with salt, pepper, and lemon juice. Bake for 10 minutes. Remove from oven, and use a knife to cut a small V into center and check core of meat. When the center is still slightly translucent, the tuna is cooked enough. Let stand on plate for 5 minutes to finish cooking. Serve hot. SERVES 2.
SIDE DISH SUGGESTIONS: Fresh cucumber, kiwi and mango slices.

FRESH FAR EAST TUNA BAKE

1 pound fresh tuna steak (2 portions, ½ inch thick)
1 tablespoon margarine
½ teaspoon salt
½ teaspoon pepper
½ teaspoon lemon juice
1 small onion, coarsely chopped
2 stalks celery, coarsely chopped
1 14-ounce can bean sprouts
1 8-ounce can sliced water chestnuts
½ cup teriyaki sauce

Pre-heat the oven to 425 degrees F. Coat the bottom of a medium-sized glass baking dish with margarine. Place tuna steaks in dish and sprinkle each with salt, pepper, and lemon juice. Bake for 5 minutes and remove tuna from baking dish. It will still be slightly raw in center. Place tuna on a plate to cool. Reduce heat to 350 degrees F.

Drain water from bean sprouts and water chestnuts. Coat the baking dish again with margarine and add bean sprouts, chestnuts, onion, and celery. When tuna is cool to the touch, break meat into small pieces and add to mixture. Pour in teriyaki sauce and gently mix all ingredients. Bake for 20 minutes. Serve hot.

SERVES 4 to 6.

SIDE DISH SUGGESTION: Rice with snow peas.

TUNA KEBABS

1 pound fresh skinless tuna
2 medium sweet onions
1 red, yellow, or green bell pepper
12 cherry tomatoes
6 wooden or metal skewers, 6 inches or longer
½ pound shell-on shrimp, 36-45 count or smaller (optional)
1 tablespoon soy sauce
½ teaspoon fresh ginger, chopped
½ teaspoon brown sugar
1 tablespoon water
vegetable spray

Pre-heat the grill or broiler. Peel onions and cut into eighths. Cut pepper in half, remove seeds. Cut each half into three lengthwise slices, then cut those in half to make 12 pieces. Cut fresh tuna into ½-inch cubes. (If using shrimp, remove shell, devein, and cut each shrimp in half.) Place a cherry tomato at pointed end of skewer and then pull up to ½-inch from top. Now slide one chunk of tuna up to tomato, add a slice of pepper, a piece of shrimp, and a cube of onion. Repeat until skewer is full and cap off with a cherry tomato to hold food in place. Mix soy sauce, ginger, water, and brown sugar in a flat pan and place skewers in marinade for 5 minutes. Spray grill with vegetable spray and place kebabs on grill. Baste and turn as needed. Cook for 10 minutes.

SERVES 3 to 4.

SIDE DISH SUGGESTION: Corn on the cob and potato salad.

MEDITERRANEAN BAKED TUNA NIÇOISE WITH DILL

1½ pounds fresh tuna steaks (1 inch thick)
1 yellow bell pepper
3 roma or plum tomatoes
10 niçoise or any Greek olives
vegetable spray
1 teaspoon olive oil
1 tablespoon garlic, crushed or minced
1 medium red onion, thinly sliced
1 tablespoon red wine vinegar
1 teaspoon dried dill
½ teaspoon freshly ground pepper

Pre-heat the oven to 400 degrees F. Remove seeds from bell pepper and cut into strips. Slice tomatoes into eighths. Cut olives in half. Spray a baking tray with vegetable spray and bake tuna for 12-15 minutes. While tuna is baking, select a medium skillet; add oil, garlic, onions, and vinegar and sauté for 2 minutes at medium heat. Next add bell pepper, tomatoes, dill, olives, and ground pepper. Stir as needed until vegetables are softened (about 3 minutes). Check tuna after 12 minutes. If center is pink remove it from oven. Spoon Mediterranean sauce over each steak. Center of tuna will continue to cook on plate as surface cools.

SERVES 2 to 4.

SIDE DISH SUGGESTIONS: Crusty French, Italian, or German bread, with sparkling imported water.

See also:

"Real" Fresh Tuna Salad, page 146
Fresh Tomatoes Stuffed with Tuna Salad, page 147
Chapter 17, Fun with Sushi

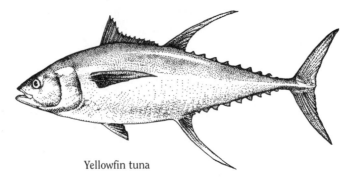

Yellowfin tuna

ISLAND FAVORITES

EASY ISLAND SEAFOOD COOKING

When the sun goes down and it is time for tropical dining, few can forget the incredible seafood dishes in the land called "Paradise."

Back on the mainland, former island visitors look forward to their next trip to the South Pacific, while others sift through island travel brochures planning that dream vacation to Hawaii. The good news is that one doesn't need to count the days until vacation time to enjoy the most popular seafood served in Hawaii. Three favorite island fish can be purchased at your nearby supermarket and easily prepared in your own home. Your family can have great fun preparing these dishes in the home as part of a Hawaiian dinner. You can grill, bake, or broil a wonderful tropical seafood main dish and enjoy a variety of favorite tropical fruits for dessert. Fresh pineapple, guava, mango, and papaya, along with several types of island fish, can be found in most supermarkets.

Since there are few major rivers or lakes in Hawaii, the ocean has been the primary source of seafood for the inhabitants of the islands. There are nearly 600 species of fish living in this great aquatic region.

The three most commonly served species of fish in the islands are dolphinfish (mahi-mahi), wahoo (ono), and ruby snapper (onaga). Mahi-mahi can be found in most supermarkets. Wahoo can also be found in the grocery store, but may not be available in all areas of the country. However, this fish is very close in taste to mahi-mahi, which can be substituted in recipes for wahoo. Ruby snapper can easily be found in most supermarket seafood counters.

Most of the fish served in Hawaii tend to be firm fleshed and therefore perfect for the grill. When placed on the grill, they tend to hold firmly in place even when being turned, like a steak or chicken. But you can also use aluminum foil or a fish-grilling pan designed to keep seafood from falling through the grill grates.

ABOUT THE FISH

Mahi-mahi is the single most popular fish served in Hawaii. It has firm flesh and grills beautifully. The meat cooks to a sweet-tasting, white-colored delicacy. Mahi-mahi can be prepared easily with a variety of cooking methods. Mahi-mahi are fast swimmers and live for about 5 years. They grow very quickly, reaching a length of 3 feet in one year and ultimately growing to as much as 5 feet, 90 pounds. Because of its rapid growth cycle, mahi-mahi is being studied now as a candidate for farm raising at sea (aquaculture).

Wahoo also has sweet, flaky firm flesh and cooks to a nice white color. It works wonderfully on the grill. Wahoo also grows rapidly, up to 44 inches and 16 pounds in one year. They can reach a maximum size of 6 feet, 180 pounds, during their 20-year life span.

Ruby snapper is considered one of the most delicate, flavorful fish from the sea. The skin is red and the meat is white. The ruby snapper lives to be about 20 years old and reaches a maximum size of 3 feet, 35 pounds. There are many other red-skinned fish that sometimes are offered for sale as ruby or red snapper. Any species of snapper would work well for the recipes in this chapter (other types of snapper sell for considerably less then true ruby or red snapper).

SELECTING AND STORING
FRESH TROPICAL ISLAND FISH

Use your eyes: Look for fish that has a nice shine to the meat. Good, freshly cut mahi-mahi will have a center bloodline that should be red or burgundy. The skin side (if it is not skinless) will be shades of gray, yellow, and greenish blue. These colors begin to fade the longer the fish has been out of the ocean. Wahoo will be pinkish gray in meat color. Ruby or red snapper meat will be creamy or white; the skin has patterns of bright red.

Smell: Ask to smell the fish. There should be no offensive fishy smell. If very fresh or freshly thawed, it will smell clean and neutral.

Touch: Ask the salesperson to press down on the skin side of the fish. If the fish is very fresh, the finger mark will spring back quickly. If old, it will stay pressed down.

Keep it cold: It is important to keep your seafood purchase as cold as possible. It is a good idea to return home directly after buying seafood and place your fish in the refrigerator to maintain the good cold temperature until time to cook. This will keep your seafood in top condition and allow you to keep it at least 2 days before cooking, if needed, without having to freeze it.

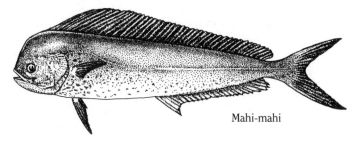

Mahi-mahi

GRILLED HONOLULU MAHI-MAHI

2 10-ounce slices of mahi-mahi
2 tablespoons soy sauce
2 tablespoons corn oil
2 tablespoons water
½ bunch scallions, finely chopped
1 teaspoon fresh ginger, finely chopped
1 lemon

Select bright, fresh mahi-mahi from the seafood counter. Pre-heat the grill. Combine soy, water, oil, scallions, ginger, and a squeeze of lemon in small saucepan. Bring to a boil and remove from heat. Cook mahi-mahi on the grill, meat-side down, for about 7 minutes. Turn and coat top with marinade. Allow about 7 minutes of cooking time.

Carefully flake center of fish with fork to see if meat has turned white and is firm. If white, remove from grill. Allow 1 to 2 minutes more cooking time if needed. Garnish with thin slices of lemon.
SERVES 2.
SIDE DISH SUGGESTIONS: Long grain wild rice, French style string beans, sweet Hawaiian bread, and fresh pineapple.

TIKI LUAU SWEET AND SOUR MAHI-MAHI KEBOBS

1½ pounds mahi-mahi (skinless)
1 fresh pineapple
2 red or yellow bell peppers
2 green bell peppers
2 large onions
12 large mushrooms
6 6- to 8-inch wooden or metal skewers
1 tablespoon sesame seeds

Sweet and sour sauce

1 tablespoon soy sauce
1 teaspoon brown sugar
1 cup tomato sauce or ketchup
1 teaspoon chopped garlic
1 teaspoon vinegar
1 teaspoon peanut oil

Pre-heat the grill. Cut mahi-mahi into 1-inch cubes. Core pineapple and cut into 1-inch cubes. Remove seeds from bell peppers and slice each into ½-inch slices. Peel onions and quarter each. Place a mushroom on skewer and slide up to about 1 inch from top. Next add a cube of mahi, a piece each of red (yellow) pepper, onion, pineapple, and green pepper. Repeat until skewer is filled; repeat with other skewers. Mix all ingredients for sweet and sour sauce. Brush each kebob with sauce and grill for 5 to 7 minutes. Brush additional sauce onto each kebob as it cooks. Remove food from grill; sprinkle each with sesame seeds and serve.
SERVES 2 to 4.
SIDE DISH SUGGESTIONS: Fresh tropical fruit and steamed rice.

BAKED MOLOKAI WAHOO

If wahoo is not available, substitute mahi-mahi, which is similar in taste and texture. Swordfish or fresh tuna may also be used.

2 10-ounce slices of wahoo
3 tablespoons mayonnaise
¼ teaspoon cayenne pepper
¼ teaspoon fresh chives, finely chopped
rind of 1 lemon

Preheat oven to 425 degrees F. Mix mayonnaise and cayenne pepper. Spread over top of wahoo fillet. Bake for about 15 minutes. Flake center

with a fork to check to see whether meat is white. Return to heat for additional 2 minutes if needed. Garnish top after cooking with a few lines of chives and thin slices of lemon rind.
SERVES 2.
SIDE DISH SUGGESTIONS: Potato soup and sweet Hawaiian bread.

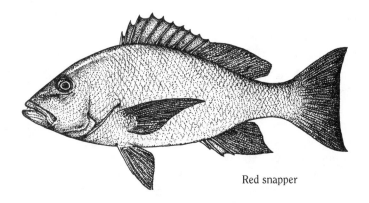

Red snapper

GRILLED TROPICAL SNAPPER TERIYAKI

2 10-ounce slices ruby or red snapper
2 tablespoons teriyaki sauce
⅓ cup scallions, finely chopped
⅓ cup carrot, shredded
1 tablespoon corn oil
1 tablespoon water
1 lemon

Pre-heat the grill. Combine teriyaki sauce, oil, water, scallions, carrots, and a squeeze of lemon in small saucepan. Bring to a boil, then remove from heat. Finish cooking side dishes. Place fish on grill and cook, meat-side down, for about 5 minutes. Turn and cover top with teriyaki marinade. Cook for about 10 minutes. Flake center with fork to test for doneness. Remove from grill or cook additional 2 minutes if needed. Garnish plate with thin slices of lemon.
SERVES 2.
SIDE DISH SUGGESTIONS: Asparagus, sweet Hawaiian bread, and fresh pineapple.

SOUTH PACIFIC STEAMED SNAPPER

1½ pounds snapper fillets, skin on (preferably red snapper)
2 cups water
1 tablespoon white distilled vinegar
1 tablespoon fresh grated ginger
1 tablespoon soy sauce
2 green onions, sliced thin
6 ounces frozen snow peas
1 tablespoon peanut oil
1 green chile pepper, 2 to 4 inches long, very finely chopped

Use a large bamboo steamer or select a pot large enough to allow a colander to rest two inches from the bottom of the pot. Pour water and vinegar in pot and bring to a rolling boil. Place fish on a cutting board and use a sharp knife to score the meat with ¼-inch diagonal lines. Set fillets around colander skin side down and place colander in the pot. Mix ginger and soy sauce and pour over each scored fillet. Garnish tops of each fillet with onions and snow peas. Cover pot and steam fish for 8 to 10 minutes. Remove fish from steam; place on serving dishes and set aside. In a small skillet heat oil and chopped chile pepper until the oil just begins to smoke. Drizzle hot oil and chile over each fillet and serve.
SERVES 2 to 4.

SIDE DISH SUGGESTION: Fresh sliced tropical fruit.

THE COD FAMILY

FISHING FOR COD

The first cod fishery was started in Portugal. In European countries cod has been an important food source for more than 500 years. Dried and salted cod provided an essential food supply for early seafarers crossing the Atlantic. Soon after the landing at Plymouth Rock, colonial America made Atlantic cod *(Gadus morhua)* a household name. This single species of fish became one of the first American natural resources. No doubt the Pilgrims were delighted to discover a rich cod resource just miles off the New England coast, an area that later became known as the richest fishing grounds in the world.

For many centuries, cod was an affordable fish. Midway through the twentieth century, however, enormous global population growth and the demand for more food caused cod prices to soar. As the demand increased, the pressure on the resource depleted its abundance. The stocks collapsed, leaving many North American fishing towns in ruin. With modern scientific knowledge and government intervention, the resource has slowly begun to rebound. Nearly one-third of all fresh fish fillet and half of all the fish sticks and fish portions consumed in the United States today are still made from cod.

COUSINS OF THE COD

Cod is part of a family of fish, *Gadidae*, that are fished in the northern waters of the Atlantic and the Pacific. There are several fish in this group that have fairly similar appearance and a taste that allows them to be good substitutes for cod.

Is it "cod" or is it "scrod"? People become very confused over these terms. Yet be assured, either way the fish is still cod. The term "scrod" actually refers to fillet cut from small codfish (3 pounds or smaller). As the fish increase in size the terms change to "cod" and "market cod." In most parts of the world, the fish is simply "cod." While traveling through New England you will hear "scrod" more often. This can also refer to a small haddock, in which case the spelling may be "schrod."

The remaining fish that make up the cod family look similar to the Atlantic and Pacific cod when in whole live form. Once cut into fillet or steak, some may appear identical. For this reason, the haddock, which is premium-priced fish, often is sold skin-on. Once the skin is removed, even a fish expert would have difficulty determining if it is cod or haddock.

Atlantic cod

Related species

> Red hake, silver hake (Atlantic whiting)
> Pollack (Atlantic and Alaskan)
> Haddock (considered the premium cod-family fish)
> Lingcod (greenling family)

Any of these fish can be used successfully in any cod recipe, or where white, mild flaky fish is required. Cod is an excellent diet fish, for it has less than 1 gram of fat per 3.5-ounce raw serving. With its unique leanness and neutral flavor, cod works well as a substitute in dishes where more expensive, heavily seasoned fish is normally used. For example, high-quality cod, frozen at sea and freshly thawed, can double for blue crabmeat when made into a crab cake. These fish cook very fast and fit any cooking method, especially those using moist heat.

BROILED CODFISH OR HAKE STEAKS

1½ pounds fresh cod or hake steaks, cut at least 1 inch thick
¼ teaspoon garlic, finely chopped
½ teaspoon onion, minced
1 teaspoon olive oil
1 tablespoon mayonnaise
1 teaspoon lemon-pepper seasoning
2 tablespoons fresh parsley, finely chopped
vegetable spray

Have the steaks cut at least 1 inch thick. Pre-heat the broiler. Mix garlic, onion, oil, and mayonnaise. Brush steaks with sauce. Sprinkle with lemon-pepper seasoning and top with parsley. Spray broiler tray with vegetable spray. Place steaks on broiler pan and cook for 7 to 10 minutes. Check center of one steak with a fork to see that it flakes easily. Remove from heat and serve.

SERVES 2.

SIDE DISH SUGGESTIONS: Sour cream and fresh crunchy veggies (broccoli, carrot sticks, celery, tomatoes).

EASY MICROWAVE COD FILLETS

Microwaved seafood is quick and easy. Since most seafood, especially finfish, is 60 to 80 percent water, the microwave tends to be a great cooking method. The two key elements to making perfect fish are rotation during cooking and keeping the food covered to prevent dehydration. Average cooking time for most seafood is about 3 minutes at high heat.

1 pound fresh or frozen cod fillets
4 pats of butter
½ teaspoon lemon-pepper seasoning
¼ cup flavored bread crumbs

Place fillets skin-side down on a dish on a microwave-rotating disc. Cut butter pats in two and dress each fillet with several pieces along meat. Microwave on high for 30 seconds to melt butter. Remove from oven. Sprinkle with seasoning and bread crumbs. Cover with plastic wrap, return to microwave oven, and cook at high heat for 2½ minutes. Check center of fish by flaking with a fork to see if meat is white.

SERVES 2.

SIDE DISH SUGGESTIONS: French style string beans and mashed potatoes.

SCROD/COD MARINARA

2 pounds cod or scrod fillets
1 medium onion, finely chopped
1 clove garlic, finely chopped
1 small sweet green pepper, finely chopped
1 28-ounce can crushed Italian tomatoes
¼ cup olive oil
1 tablespoon oregano
1 bay leaf
1 teaspoon Parmesan cheese
1 pound linguini
vegetable spray

Pre-heat the oven to 325 degrees F. In a saucepan, combine onion, garlic, sweet pepper, and oil and sauté for 5 minutes or until onions are translucent. Add tomatoes, oregano, and bay leaf, and sauté 5 minutes longer. Add grated cheese and stir. Start cooking linguini according to the instructions on the package. Cut fish fillets into 3-inch portions. Spray a baking dish with vegetable spray and gently place fish in dish. Pour marinara sauce over fillets and bake for 15 minutes. When linguini is cooked, remove from pot, drain, and divide in portions on serving dishes. Remove baked fish from the oven. Using a spatula, gently lift the fish from the sauce and place onto linguini on each plate. Remove bay leaf and discard. Spoon on sauce and serve.
SERVES 4 to 6.
SIDE DISH SUGGESTIONS: Garlic bread and fresh olives.

TRADITIONAL NEW ENGLAND
BATTER-DIPPED FRIED COD

2 pounds fresh or frozen cod or cod family fillets
1 cup flour
½ teaspoon salt
½ teaspoon pepper
2 eggs
1 cup milk
2 cups olive or other vegetable oil

Sift flour into a large deep bowl. Sprinkle with salt and pepper. Beat eggs and milk until yellow and pour into the flour. Whisk mixture until batter is well blended. Place cod fillet on cutting board. Run fingers carefully along fillet and feel for bones. (A fillet is not necessarily boneless; always check.) Remove any bones with tweezers or knife. Cut the fillet into three portions. In a deep frying pan, heat oil on high heat. Dip fillets into batter, allowing a few seconds for excess to run off, and place in hot oil. Turn fillets gently to brown all sides. Once the batter is golden brown, remove a fillet from the heat and cut in half to inspect. The meat should be snowy white. If still translucent, continue cooking a minute or two longer. Thicker pieces of fish will take longer.

SERVES 3 to 5.

SIDE DISH SUGGESTIONS: French fries and coleslaw.

BELLA BACCULA (SALTED COD)

1 pound salted cod (whole fillets)
6 cups of water
2 medium onions, minced
1 teaspoon garlic, crushed or minced
2 tablespoons olive oil
½ cup white wine
½ teaspoon black pepper
1 can diced tomatoes
8 ounces your favorite tomato sauce
1 green bell pepper

Soak salted cod fillets in 6 cups of water for 24 hours in refrigerator. Change water 3 times during the period. The next day, drain cod and squeeze fish to remove as much water as possible.

Pre-heat the oven to 325 degrees F. Sauté onion and garlic in oil at medium heat until soft. Reduce heat to low and stir in wine, black pepper, and tomatoes. Simmer for 15 minutes. Place fillets in a single layer in a wide baking dish. Pour tomato sauce over fish, slice green pepper thin, and garnish top of dish. Bake for 20 minutes. Check center of one fillet with a fork to be sure it is flaky. Remove from oven and serve.

SERVES: 4 to 6.

SIDE DISH SUGGESTIONS: Pasta, salad, and bread.

BACCULA CAKES (SALTED COD)

1 pound dried salted cod (or dried cod bits)
6 cups water
2 medium onions, minced
2 tablespoons butter
1 egg
1 teaspoon salt
1 teaspoon pepper
1 teaspoon dried parsley
1 teaspoon seafood seasoning
1 slice bread
1 cup flour
¼ cup cornmeal
2 cups vegetable oil

Soak salted cod in 6 cups of water for 24 hours in refrigerator. Change water 3 times during that period. The next day, drain cod and squeeze fish to remove as much water as possible. Shred fish with a knife. Sauté onions with butter at low heat until soft.

In a large bowl beat egg. Mix in cod, onions, salt, pepper, parsley, seafood seasoning, and crumbled bread. Blend flour and cornmeal on a large sheet of wax paper. Pre-heat the oil in same skillet used for onions. Make fish into cakes. Dredge each in flour and fry until golden brown.

SERVES: 4 TO 6 PEOPLE
SIDE DISH SUGGESTIONS: Baked beans and ketchup.

COD, HADDOCK, LING, HAKE, OR POLLACK A LA KING

1 pound fish fillets
¼ cup butter
1 cup fresh mushrooms, finely chopped
1 green bell pepper, finely chopped
¼ cup pimento, chopped
1 cup milk
¼ cup flour
1 cup peas
vegetable spray

Sauce: Melt butter in a saucepan at medium heat. Sauté chopped vegetables until soft. Add flour, milk, and peas. Cover pot and simmer for 3 minutes.

Spray broiler tray with vegetable spray. Place fillets on broiler pan and cook for 7 to 10 minutes. Check center of one steak with a fork to see that it flakes easily. Remove from heat, place on serving dish, cover with sauce, and serve.

SERVES 2.

SIDE DISH SUGGESTION: Buttered egg noodles.

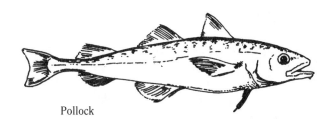

Pollock

FISH CAKES AND BOSTON BAKED BEANS, GLOUCESTER STYLE

1 pound fresh or freshly thawed cod fillets
2 cups water
2 slices dry bread
½ bunch fresh parsley, finely chopped
¼ teaspoon salt
¼ teaspoon pepper
1 egg
2 tablespoons mayonnaise
2 cups flour
½ cup vegetable oil

Place cod on cutting board and run fingers carefully along fillets and feel for bones. (A fillet is not necessarily boneless; always check.) Remove any bones with tweezers or knife. Bring 2 cups of water to a boil in a large pot. Place a colander in the pot and layer fish along sides. Steam fish until it turns white. Remove from heat, allow cooling, and flake into pieces in a large mixing bowl. Crumble dry bread over cod and sprinkle with parsley, salt, and pepper. In a small bowl whisk egg and mayonnaise, then pour over cod. Mix gently with hands. Shape into tight, flat, 2-inch cakes. Place flour on a large sheet of wax paper; roll each fish cake in flour. Add oil to skillet, place on medium heat, and fry cakes until golden. Turn as needed.

SERVES 3 to 4.

SIDE DISH SUGGESTIONS: Boston-style baked beans and ketchup.

BROILED HADDOCK WITH HONEY-LIME SAUCE

1 pound haddock fillets, skin on (or substitute skinless cod)
1 tablespoon honey
3 teaspoons freshly squeezed lime juice
1 tablespoon olive oil
¼ teaspoon red pepper
¼ teaspoon grated lime peel
½ teaspoon dry parsley

Mix honey, lime juice, oil, pepper, and lime peel in a large bowl. Cut haddock fillets into individual portions and place in bowl with marinade. Refrigerate for 15 minutes, stirring several times to mix in marinade. Pre-heat the broiler. Place fish portions skin side down on broiler tray and broil about 4 inches from heat. Broil for 5 minutes and spoon remaining marinade over top of fillets. Broil for 3 more minutes. Remove from heat, flake center of a fillet with a fork, and if white, serve. Garnish with sprinkles of parsley.

SERVES 2 to 3.

SIDE DISH SUGGESTIONS: Crusty bread with pesto.

HADDOCK MORNAY

2 pounds haddock fillets (skin removed)
3¼ cups half-and-half
2 tablespoons butter
¼ teaspoon onion powder
½ teaspoon salt
¼ cup flour
2 egg yolks
¼ cup Swiss cheese, grated
vegetable spray

Pre-heat the broiler. In a small saucepan add half-and-half and butter and cook at low heat until butter is melted. Add onion powder and salt and whisk in flour. Cook sauce until it thickens, stirring constantly. Beat egg yolks and slowly add to the sauce, stirring. When sauce is just about to bubble, mix in cheese and remove from heat.

Spray broiler pan with vegetable spray and place fillets on tray in a single layer. Broil 4 inches from heat for 12 minutes.

Flake center of fillet with a fork to be sure fish is cooked. Place fillets on serving dishes and pour mornay sauce generously over each fillet.
SERVES 4 to 6.
SIDE DISH SUGGESTIONS: Asparagus and boiled potatoes.

FINNAN HADDIE

1½ pounds smoked haddock or cod
1 cup milk
¼ pound butter
3 eggs
1 cup heavy cream
1 teaspoon pepper
2 tablespoons flour
¼ cup water

Hard boil the eggs, cool, and slice. Warm milk in a skillet at low heat. When milk is beginning to bubble, place smoked fillets in liquid to soften meat. Poach fish for 1½ minutes, and then remove from milk. Melt butter in a saucepan. Flake the smoked fish and combine fish, eggs, heavy cream and pepper in saucepan. Mix flour and water in a cup and then pour into pot. Stir until Finnan Haddie thickens. Serve on toast or hot buttered biscuits.
SERVES: 4 to 6.
SIDE DISH SUGGESTION: Other breakfast foods.

See also: **Gloucester Fish Chowder,** page 143

FLOUNDER AND SOLE

RIGHT-EYED AND LEFT-EYED FLATFISH

Depending on where you live, this fish will be called a flounder or a sole. The general category is simply flatfish, for they are just that. Adult flounder and sole have eyes on only the top of their bodies, but begin their life with one eye on each side. As the flatfish gets older, its eyes move together to the upper side. Flounder and sole are described as being left-eyed or right-eyed, referring to the direction that the eyes face when the fish swims. There are over 530 species of flounder. Species of flounder or sole can be found in all the oceans of the world. Most are relatively small fish weighing between 2 and 4 pounds.

Flounder and sole rank high in seafood consumption statistics, falling just below tuna, shrimp, and salmon. One of the most attractive characteristics of flatfish is their bone structure. These fish can be filleted cleanly from the bone, producing a virtually boneless piece of fish. Since flounder is white flaky meat and has an extremely mild flavor, most restaurants offer some type on their menus. It is one of the most popular fish to be cooked in the home.

Flatfish have a dark skin side and a white skin side. The dark side faces up and away from the ocean bottom and is used to camouflage the fish. Flounder and sole can change colors to match the ocean floor. When the skin is removed, some fillets will have a darker side, and others will be whiter. The skin side will usually have a shiny look. It is best to cook flat fish skin-side down. Because the fish are so thin, it is rarely necessary to turn the fillet when cooking.

THE NINE MOST COMMON COMMERCIAL SPECIES

Sea Dabs: American plaice, North Atlantic, right-eyed
West Coast Dover sole: Pacific flounder, Pacific Ocean, right-eyed
(The only true Dover sole is found in the Mediterranean and North Sea.)
Gray sole: witch flounder, North Atlantic, left-eyed
Lemon sole: winter flounder, North Atlantic, right-eyed
Rock sole: rock flounder, Pacific Ocean, right-eyed
Yellow Tail: North Atlantic, right-eyed
Fluke: summer flounder, North Atlantic, left-eyed
Turbot: mainly North Atlantic and Greenland area; averaging 3 feet, up to 30 pounds
Halibut: North Atlantic and Pacific; largest of all flatfish, up to 9 feet, 700 pounds

How to fillet a flounder

With the eye side up, make an incision along the spine from the gills to the tail.

Slide the blade between the backbone and the flesh. Lift the fillet making sure the bones stay in place.

Turn the fish over and repeat the previous step.

FISH AND CHIPS, ENGLISH STYLE

1 pound flounder/sole fillets
1 cup flour
½ teaspoon salt
½ teaspoon pepper
2 eggs
1 cup milk
2 cups olive or other vegetable oil
4 large potatoes, skin-on

Sift flour into a large deep bowl. Sprinkle with salt and pepper. Beat eggs and milk until yellow. Gradually add flour to liquid. Whisk mixture until batter is well blended. Place flounder/sole fillets on cutting board. Cut in half lengthwise, then cut these pieces in half. Flounder is very thin, so it cooks fast. Add oil to deep frying pan and place on high heat. Rinse potatoes, dry, and slice into thin fries (do not remove skin). Place fries in hot oil and cook until golden. When fries are out of the hot oil, turn heat to medium. Dip fillets in batter and fry them until golden. The fish will take one-third less time to cook than the fries, so the potatoes will still be hot when the meal is ready.
SERVES 3 to 5.
SIDE DISH SUGGESTIONS: Vinegar, ketchup, and lemonade.

ALMOND-MUSHROOM TANGY FLOUNDER FILLETS

1½ pounds flounder fillets
2 cups vegetable oil
1 egg
¼ cup milk
1 cup flour
1 lemon
1 teaspoon salt
1 teaspoon pepper
1 10-ounce can cream of mushroom soup
¼ cup toasted almonds, slivered

Pre-heat skillet with oil at medium/high heat. Mix egg and milk in a bowl. Dip fillets in batter and dredge in flour. Sprinkle with salt, pepper, and a squeeze of lemon and fry until golden. Drain oil from pan and cover fish with cream of mushroom soup straight from the can. Sprinkle with almonds. Cover pan and cook in microwave at medium heat for 2 minutes. Serve over steamed rice or egg noodles.
SERVES 2 to 4.
SIDE DISH SUGGESTIONS: String beans and carrots.

FLOUNDER FLORENTINE

    1½ pounds flounder/sole fillets
    10-ounce package frozen chopped spinach
    ¼ cup milk
    1 tablespoon melted butter
    4 tablespoons grated Parmesan cheese
    3 tablespoons plain bread crumbs
    vegetable spray

Florentine: Fill a one-quart pot with hot tap water, bring to boil, and add frozen spinach. Cook until spinach is separated, rinse under cold running water, and drain well. In a medium-sized mixing bowl, combine spinach, cold milk, melted butter, Parmesan cheese, and bread crumbs. Mix until Florentine is semi-stiff.

Place a very thin coat of vegetable spray in baking dish. Arrange flounder or sole fillet in a single layer in baking dish, meat-side up. Spread a ½-inch layer of Florentine over top. Bake at 350 degrees F for 5 to 7 minutes. Serve hot.

SERVES 3 to 5.

SIDE DISH SUGGESTIONS: Mashed potatoes and cornbread.

FLOUNDER ALMANDINE

    1½ pounds flounder or sole fillets
    1 egg
    ¼ cup milk
    ¼ teaspoon salt
    ¼ teaspoon pepper
    1 cup flour
    ½ cup butter
    2 tablespoons fresh parsley, finely chopped
    ½ cup sliced almonds

Mix egg, milk, salt, and pepper in a deep bowl. Place fillets in bowl, and let stand for 2 minutes. Sift flour onto a dish or waxed paper. Remove fillets and dredge them in the flour. In a large frying pan, melt butter at medium heat and then sauté fillets 2 to 3 minutes or until golden. Turn gently only if needed. Remove fish from pan, and reduce heat to low. Place portions of fish on serving dishes. In the same pan sauté almonds and parsley for 1½ minutes. Spoon almonds, parsley, and butter remaining in the pan over each fish portion. Serve hot.

SERVES 3 to 4.

SIDE DISH SUGGESTIONS: Rice pilaf and asparagus.

WHOLE FLOUNDER, THAI STYLE

  2 medium-sized whole flounders (or other small white-fleshed
      fish, 1 to 1½ pounds each)
  2 carrots
  1 13½-ounce can coconut milk
  2 teaspoons brown sugar
  1 tablespoon lemon juice
  1 bunch scallions, finely chopped
  1 tablespoon ginger, finely chopped
  1 tablespoon garlic, crushed or minced
  3 eggs
  2 cups vegetable oil
  1 tablespoon curry powder
  1 cup flour

Slice carrots thin julienne style. In a saucepan mix ½ can coconut milk, carrots, sugar, lemon juice, scallions, ginger, and garlic, and bring to a boil at medium heat. Reduce heat to low and cook for 2 minutes. Remove sauce from heat and set aside. Mix eggs and ½ can of coconut milk. Pre-heat oil in a large skillet at medium/high heat to 350 degrees F. Mix curry powder into flour and spread flour on cutting board or waxed paper. Dip flounder into batter and dredge in flour. Dip flounder in batter again and apply second coat of flour for extra crispness. Deep-fry flounder until golden. Re-heat Thai sauce for 2 minutes. Drain excess oil from fish. Place each fish on a serving plate, score the top by cutting deep diagonal lines with a sharp knife, and spoon sauce over top of fish.
SERVES 2 to 4.
SIDE DISH SUGGESTION: Steamed white rice.

BALTIC FLOUNDER ROLL-UPS

  1½ pounds flounder fillets
  ½ cup butter
  1 teaspoon salt
  1 teaspoon pepper
  1 tablespoon dry parsley
  1 egg
  ¼ cup milk
  1½ cups flour
  1 cup vegetable oil

Cut butter into ¼-inch pats. Place a pat of butter at one end of each fillet. Sprinkle fillet with salt, pepper, and dry parsley. Roll the fillet tightly around the butter. Mix egg and milk in a bowl. Dip each fillet in egg-milk mixture and roll in flour. Squeeze the edges of the fillet gently between both hands to form a pastry turnover look. Re-dip roll-ups in batter as needed, apply more flour and squeeze again to seal the fillet edges. Place roll-ups in refrigerator until ready to prepare meal. Allow at least ½ hour to chill. Then heat oil in skillet to 350 degrees F at medium/high. Dredge cold roll-ups in flour and fry until golden.
SERVES 2 to 4.
SIDE DISH SUGGESTION: French-style string beans and long grain wild rice.

FLOUNDER STUFFED WITH CRABMEAT

  1½ pounds flounder fillets
  8 ounces blue or snow crabmeat
  2 tablespoons butter
  ¼ cup celery, finely chopped
  ¼ cup onion, finely chopped
  1 egg
  3 tablespoons mayonnaise
  ¼ teaspoon mustard
  ¼ teaspoon seafood seasoning
  3 soda crackers, crushed
  vegetable spray

Melt butter in a skillet, add celery and onion and cook until soft. In a bowl, mix egg, mayonnaise, mustard, seafood seasoning, crabmeat, celery, onion, and crushed crackers. Pre-heat oven to 350 degrees F. Place flounder fillets on a cutting board. Make a meatball-sized portion of stuffing. Place stuffing at one end of a flounder fillet and roll fillet around the stuffing. Use a toothpick to hold wrap firm. Repeat with other fillets. Spray a baking dish with vegetable spray; place rolled fillets in dish and bake for about 15 minutes. Because flounder is thin, it will cook very fast; you will need to baste the top of the fish with butter to keep the roll-ups moist. The thicker stuffing center will take longer to heat than the fish.
SERVES 2 to 4.
SIDE DISH SUGGESTIONS: Potatoes au gratin and tossed salad.

FOIL-GRILLED GARLIC-BUTTER FLOUNDER WITH GARDEN VEGGIES

1½ pounds flounder fillets
2 fresh carrots
1 medium-sized zucchini
1 large potato
1 green bell pepper
3 large mushrooms
1 large onion
¼ cup butter
1 teaspoon garlic, crushed or minced
¼ teaspoon salt
1 tablespoon cooking sherry

Pre-heat the grill. Wash vegetables. Peel carrots, zucchini, and potato. Slice each julienne style. Remove seeds from pepper and cut fish and peppers into 3-inch pieces. Thinly slice mushrooms and onion. Cut a 2-foot length of aluminum foil and draw edges upward to form a bowl-like structure. Place flounder, vegetables, butter, garlic, sherry, and salt inside pocket, and then bring all sides together and crimp closed, leaving an air pocket inside. Grill foil pouch for 15 minutes. Remove from heat and serve.

SERVES 2 to 4.

SIDE DISH SUGGESTIONS: Hot apple slices and bread.

SWORDFISH AND HALIBUT

THE GREAT GRILLING FAVORITES

Grilling fish on the BBQ grill is a wonderful experience. In coastal areas where seafood is a regular part of the weekly menu plan, grilled fish is often a summertime favorite. Two of the best tasting and easiest fish to grill are swordfish and halibut. You can learn how to master these great grill favorites in your backyard and enjoy an elegant tasting, restaurant quality dish in your own home. Swordfish, otherwise referred to as billfish, are found in oceans worldwide. The swordfish is a single species *(Xiphias gladius)*. These fast-swimming fish can weigh over 1,000 pounds and are caught on a long line and traditional "Old World" style harpoon. In 1998, concerns about over-fishing of swordfish in the North Atlantic sparked boycotts by restaurant owners and cruise ships. Thus far, research data have failed to provide undisputed evidence of an immediate need for severe conservation measures.

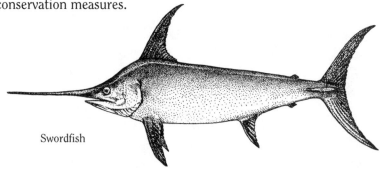

Swordfish

The swordfish in your area supermarket or fish store can be fresh or frozen. Most fresh product comes from Chile or Hawaii. The frozen-at-sea product, known as "clipper," is imported from Japan or Singapore. Swordfish is always sold in steak form and can be cut to the thickness you desire. This fish has a rich, slightly sweet flavor and a dense texture like that of beefsteak or tuna. It has a high oil content and is rich in omega-3 fatty acids.

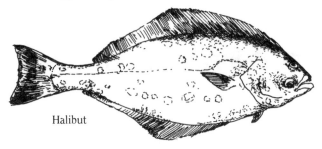

Halibut

Halibut is the largest of all the flatfish, with record fish reaching 9 feet in length and 700 pounds. Fishermen call these "whales." Steaks sold in your market are cut from fish weighing 10 to 150 pounds. Halibut is harvested mainly in the Bering Sea around Alaska; a very limited amount is fished in the Atlantic. Halibut is sold mostly in steaks with the skin on in both fresh and frozen form. Its mild flavor and firm meat make it excellent for grilling.

To maintain moisture in your swordfish and halibut, select steaks that are cut a minimum of 1 to 1¼ inches thick.

GRILLED SWORDFISH KEBABS POLYNESIAN

1 pound swordfish steak
½ cup sweet and sour sauce
1 tablespoon soy sauce
¼ teaspoon fresh ginger, finely minced or grated
1 large onion
2 green bell peppers
1 fresh pineapple
12 cherry tomatoes
6 10-inch wooden or metal skewers
vegetable spray

Pre-heat the grill. Mix sweet and sour sauce, soy sauce, and ginger in a bowl. Cut swordfish into 1-inch cubes and place in bowl of sauce for 5 minutes. Peel onion and cut into 6 sections. Cut peppers in half;

remove seeds and slice into six pieces each. Core pineapple, and cut into 1-inch cubes. Place a tomato on skewer and slide up to 1 inch from the top. Place a swordfish cube on skewer and slide up to tomato. Add a piece of onion, pineapple, and pepper. Repeat until skewer is full. Finish with a cherry tomato to hold food on stick. Spray grill with vegetable spray and place kebabs on grill. Brush sauce over each as needed. Cook 7 minutes. Remove from grill and serve hot.
SERVES 3 to 5.
SIDE DISH SUGGESTIONS: Steamed rice and Chinese vegetables.

MISSIONARY'S SWORDFISH CHILI

1 pound swordfish steak
4 tablespoons chili powder
1 squeeze fresh lemon
1 cup milk
1 tablespoon oil
1 sweet green pepper, diced
1 jalapeño pepper
1 medium onion, diced
1 29-ounce can tomato sauce
½ teaspoon Tabasco sauce
2 teaspoons salt
4½ cups water
2 15-ounce cans kidney beans
¼ cup flour
¼ cup cheddar cheese, shredded

Dice swordfish; sprinkle with 1 tablespoon chili powder and squeeze of lemon and soak in milk for 20 minutes. Pre-heat oil in a deep pot at medium heat and sauté sweet pepper, jalapeño pepper, and onion until soft. Drain milk from swordfish and add fish to simmering vegetables. Cook until fish turns white. Add tomato sauce, Tabasco sauce, chili powder, salt, and 4 cups of water; cook at medium heat for 5 minutes. Reduce heat to low, cover the pot, and simmer for 30 minutes. Add kidney beans to the chili. Taste chili and add more chili powder or Tabasco sauce as needed to make chili as hot as you like. Mix flour with ½ cup water and stir into chili to thicken. Serve chili in bowls and garnish each with shredded cheddar cheese.
SERVES 4 to 6.
SIDE DISH SUGGESTIONS: Steamed rice and cornbread.

GRILLED SWORDFISH TERIYAKI STEAKS

4 swordfish steaks, 1 inch thick
1 cup crushed pineapple
1 green bell pepper, finely chopped
1 teaspoon garlic, crushed or chopped
½ teaspoon ginger, finely chopped or grated
1 tablespoon brown sugar
½ cup cooking sherry
1 teaspoon soy sauce
vegetable spray

Pre-heat the grill. In a small saucepan mix pineapple, chopped pepper, garlic, ginger, sugar, sherry, and soy sauce. Sauté at medium heat until vegetables are soft. Remove from heat and cover swordfish steaks with sauce. Allow fish to marinate for 5 minutes. Spray grill with vegetable spray. Place steaks on grill and cook each side for 5 minutes. Apply sauce as needed to keep fish moist. Check center of one steak by flaking with a fork. If center is white, remove from heat and serve. SERVES 4.
SIDE DISH SUGGESTIONS: Baked potato and garlic bread.

BAKED SWORDFISH WITH SPICY MUSTARD

1 pound swordfish steaks (¾ inch or thicker)
2 scallions, finely chopped
1 tablespoon stone-ground mustard
1 tablespoon soy sauce
1 tablespoon olive oil
1 teaspoon brown sugar
1 teaspoon red wine vinegar
vegetable spray

Pre-heat the oven to 400 degrees F. Mix scallions, mustard, soy sauce, oil, sugar, and vinegar. Baste one side of steaks with spicy mustard marinade. Let stand for 5 minutes. Spray a baking tray with vegetable spray. Bake fish for 12 minutes. Switch the oven to broil and place fish 2 inches from heat and brown tops for 1 minute. Check center of a steak to see if it is cooked. If translucent in center, return to broiler for 1 to 2 minutes. SERVES 2.
SIDE DISH SUGGESTIONS: Tossed salad and baked potato.

GRILLED HALIBUT

1 pound halibut steak, 1 inch thick
½ bunch scallions, finely chopped
1 garlic clove, minced
½ teaspoon lemon juice
2 tablespoons water
¼ cup olive oil
¼ teaspoon hot sauce
vegetable spray

Pre-heat the grill. In a small saucepan combine scallions, garlic, lemon juice, water, olive oil, and hot sauce. Place on medium/high heat and cook for 3 minutes. Spray grill with vegetable oil, and place halibut steaks on grill for 1 minute to sear. Turn steaks and baste top with sauce. Grill for 4 minutes, turn steaks, baste other side and cook for 5 minutes. Flake center with fork to check meat for doneness. Remove from grill and serve hot.

SERVES 2 to 3.
SIDE DISH SUGGESTION: Fettuccini Alfredo.

SEATTLE HALIBUT WITH CHIPS

2 pounds boneless halibut
2 eggs
¼ cup water
6 tablespoons flour
1 tablespoon baking powder
¼ teaspoon salt
¼ teaspoon pepper
2 cups oil
18 frozen steak fries

Pre-heat oil in a deep pot. Mix eggs, water, flour, baking powder, salt, and pepper in a bowl. Whisk until thick and creamy. Place in refrigerator to chill while you fry steak fries until golden. When fries are cooked, remove from heat and allow excess oil to drain. Cut fish into strips about ½ inch wide. Dip the fillet strips in the batter and allow 5 seconds for excess batter to dip off. Place strips in hot oil and fry until golden brown. Remove from oil and drain.

SERVES 4 to 6.
SIDE DISH SUGGESTIONS: Coleslaw and cottage cheese.

BAKED HALIBUT WITH SHRIMP SAUCE

1 pound halibut steaks (1 inch thick)
vegetable spray

Shrimp Sauce:
1 tablespoon butter
¼ pound raw salad shrimp, finely chopped
½ cup celery, finely chopped
2 scallions, finely chopped
½ teaspoon ground mustard
1 teaspoon lemon juice
1 teaspoon salt and pepper
1 tablespoon flour
¼ cup milk

Pre-heat the oven to 450 degrees F. Spray baking tray with vegetable spray. Bake halibut for 12 minutes. While halibut is baking, make the shrimp sauce. Flake center of fish with a fork after 12 minutes and if still translucent in center, continue to bake for additional 2 to 5 minutes.

Shrimp sauce: Melt butter in a saucepan and sauté shrimp, celery, scallions, mustard, lemon juice, salt, and pepper, until vegetables are softened (about 3 minutes at medium/high heat). Whisk flour and milk and then add to sauté, stirring until thickened. When fish is cooked, spoon sauce over each steak and serve.

SERVES 2 to 4.

SIDE DISH SUGGESTIONS: Baked potato and fresh sliced cucumber.

FLORIDA GROUPER

The grouper is the largest in a family of fish known as sea bass, which includes over 400 species and inhabits temperate and tropical waters. Grouper, however, are found primarily in the Atlantic and Gulf of Mexico. A few species are fished in waters off southern California, and Hawaii has a small grouper population, mostly due to its massive coral reefs.

Because grouper seldom swim in groups (schools), they are mostly caught one at a time, on hook and line near rock piles, shipwrecks, and coral reefs. Fishing of this type, as compared to trawling nets, is labor intensive. However, the rewards are significant for fishermen and consumers. Since the fish are caught hook and line, the grouper come aboard the boat alive. Fish harvested in this fashion are less stressed. Fish caught in nets tend to thrash about and dangle sometimes for hours before being hauled aboard the vessel. When the hook and line method is used, the meat of the fish is generally of high quality, light in color, and very tasty. Of course grouper prices are reflective of premium-landed fish. The peak harvest time for grouper is summer and fall, so you can expect even higher prices other times of the year.

This chapter is titled "Florida Grouper" in recognition that nearly three-quarters of the annual commercial catch is from waters on both coasts of Florida. Red grouper and black grouper are the most common, with red being the most flavorful. Other names you may see for grouper are misty, Nassau, marbled, and Jewfish. Most of the grouper range in weight from 10 to 20 pounds. Jewfish are the largest of the family group and have been captured up to 700 pounds. These fish, due to their enormous size, are popular public aquarium specimens.

Cooking note: Grouper lends itself well to any cooking method. Since it is a very lean fish, you will want to be extra careful with your cooking time and heat intensity to avoid drying out the meat. Adding moisture by basting while cooking or marinating before frying will enhance the meat's ability to retain water.

FLORIDA STYLE SOUTHERN-FRIED GROUPER

1 pound grouper fillets
1 egg
½ cup milk
1½ cups flour
1 teaspoon any seafood seasoning
2 cups vegetable oil

Cut larger grouper fillets into portions. Rinse fillets under cold running water (do not dry). Add egg and milk to a large bowl; place fillets in liquid and let stand for 5 minutes. On a large sheet of wax paper or a dish, combine flour and seafood seasoning and blend with a spoon. Select a large skillet; add oil and place on medium/high heat. Remove fillets one-by-one and place them on flour. Gently push down on the fillet to coat the fish with flour, then turn and coat other side. For extra crispy batter, quickly re-dip fillets into liquid, and then flour each a second time. Cook each side of fillet 2 to 3 minutes. **Avoid overcooking.** Inspect center by flaking with a fork. It is better not to continue cooking than to have a fillet that is dry. Grouper makes an outstanding fish sandwich.

Homemade tartar sauce for fried fish

Tartar sauce is a tasty complement to fried fish if used in moderate amounts. Since fish has a high water content, the frying process tends to evaporate moisture quickly. The important thing when frying fish is to use moderate heat and cook slowly.

1 cup mayonnaise
1 teaspoon dill relish
½ teaspoon pepper
½ teaspoon lemon juice

Mix mayonnaise, relish, pepper and lemon. Add to top of fried fish to suit taste.

SERVES 2.

SIDE DISH SUGGESTIONS: Hush puppies or cornbread.

BROILED GROUPER

1 pound grouper fillets
vegetable spray
3 tablespoon melted butter or margarine
1 teaspoon lemon and pepper seasoning

Pre-heat the broiler. Spray broiler tray with vegetable oil. Rinse fillets under cold water. Cut grouper into portions, or leave as whole fillet. Place fish on broiler, meat side up. Grouper fillet is sold skinless; look for the darker side of the fillet where the skin was removed. Brush a thin layer of butter or margarine on top of fillet, sprinkle with lemon and pepper seasoning, and broil for 8 to 10 minutes. Baste top with butter or margarine as needed to retain moisture, and check fillets every 4 minutes. Remove fillets from heat and flake with fork to inspect center. If translucent in core, return to heat for 1 to 2 minutes more. SERVES 2.

SIDE DISH SUGGESTION: Peas and carrots with mashed potatoes.

BAKED GROUPER ITALIANO

1½ pounds grouper fillets
1 large tomato
1 green bell pepper
1 tablespoon olive oil
¼ teaspoon salt
¼ teaspoon pepper
1 teaspoon garlic powder
1 teaspoon dried oregano
1 cup shredded mozzarella cheese

Pre-heat the oven to 350 degrees F. Thinly slice tomato and bell pepper. Coat bottom of a baking dish with oil, place grouper into dish, sprinkle with salt, pepper, garlic powder, and oregano. Cover tops with cheese and garnish with slice of tomato and bell pepper. Bake for about 10 minutes. Flake center of fish with fork. Meat should be white. If still translucent, return to heat for 2 minutes. SERVES 2 to 4.

SIDE DISH SUGGESTIONS: Baked potato and string beans with almonds.

SINGAPORE STEAMED GROUPER FILLETS

1 pound grouper fillets
2 carrots
1 sweet bell pepper (red or yellow)
1 lemon
1 teaspoon soy sauce
1 teaspoon cooking sherry
2 cups water
1 clove garlic, finely chopped
1 teaspoon ginger, finely chopped
½ fresh bunch scallions, chopped

Peel carrots and thinly slice carrots, sweet bell pepper, and lemon. Mix soy sauce and cooking sherry. In a large pot bring 2 cups of water to a boil. Place a colander inside pot. Place fillets in cheesecloth. Mix carrots, peppers, garlic, ginger and scallions and place on top of fillets. Wrap fish, and layer slices of lemon over top. Gently set the fish in colander, cover the pot, and steam for 10 minutes.

SERVES 2 to 4.

SIDE DISH SUGGESTION: Steamed rice.

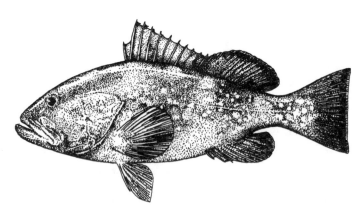

Florida grouper

MORE FINFISH

MARINATED GRILLED SHARK

1 pound shark steaks
1 tablespoon garlic, crushed or minced
1 tablespoon onion, minced
1 teaspoon salt
1 tablespoon dill, chopped
½ teaspoon black pepper, freshly ground
1 tablespoon mayonnaise
½ cup butter
½ teaspoon lemon juice
1 tablespoon fresh parsley, chopped

Pre-heat the grill. In a shallow bowl mix garlic, onion, salt, dill, pepper, and mayonnaise. Place shark steaks in bowl and marinate for 5 minutes.

Place shark on grill and brown one side for 1 minute. Turn and brush marinade over top. Cook shark for 4 minutes. Turn and brush with marinade and cook for 3 minutes. Mix butter with lemon and melt in microwave. Brush steaks with lemon-butter, turn and brown one side with lemon-butter for presentation. Remove steaks from grill and place each on a serving dish with lemon-butter side up. Garnish with chopped parsley.

SERVES 2.

SIDE DISH SUGGESTIONS: Baked beans and tossed salad.

BAKED MID-ATLANTIC BLUEFISH
WITH CRABMEAT STUFFING

2 pan-sized (1 to 1½ pounds) whole bluefish, gutted
1 pound crabmeat, cooked
2 tablespoons butter
¼ cup celery, chopped
¼ cup onion, chopped
2 eggs
¼ teaspoon mustard
4 tablespoons mayonnaise
¼ teaspoon seafood seasoning
1 slice bread
vegetable spray

Melt butter in a skillet, add celery and onion and cook until soft. In a bowl, mix eggs, mustard, mayonnaise, seafood seasoning, crabmeat, celery, onion, and crumbled bread. Pre-heat the oven to 350 degrees F. Rinse belly of fish under cold running water. Fill the clean belly cavities with stuffing. Spray a baking dish with vegetable spray. Bake fish in dish for about 20 minutes. Check stuffing by removing a sample with a fork. Stuffing only needs to be hot to taste. Then flake the meat of the fish with a fork down to the bone to be sure it is fully cooked. Add additional cooking time in 2-minute increments as needed.

SERVES 2 to 4.

SIDE DISH SUGGESTIONS: French fries and sweet peas with pearl onions.

Bluefish

BROILED BLUEFISH IMPERIAL

1½ pounds bluefish fillets, skin-on
1 egg
1 cup mayonnaise
2 tablespoon butter
1 medium onion, finely chopped
½ green bell pepper, finely chopped
½ teaspoon salt
½ teaspoon pepper
½ cup soda crackers
½ teaspoon Worcestershire sauce
vegetable spray

Pre-heat the broiler. In a saucepan melt butter and sauté onion and peppers. Beat egg, mayonnaise, salt, pepper, and Worcestershire sauce. Mix with sautéed vegetables. Spray a broiler tray with vegetable spray. Place bluefish fillets on tray, skin-side up. Broil 4 inches from heat until skin turns golden. Turn fillets gently. Coat tops of each with vegetable sauce, sprinkle with crushed crackers, and broil for 5 minutes. Check center with a fork to see if fish is flaky. Remove from heat and serve.

SERVES 2 to 4.

SIDE DISH SUGGESTIONS: Steamed broccoli and garlic mashed potatoes.

FRIED SKATE WING MEDALLIONS

2 pounds whole skinless skate wings
2 cups vegetable oil
2 eggs
¼ cup milk
1½ cups flour
1 teaspoon salt
1 teaspoon pepper
1 teaspoon seafood seasoning

Slice meat from wings and cut silver-dollar-sized medallions from each. Pre-heat oil in a large skillet at medium/high heat. Beat eggs with milk. Dip medallions into egg wash. Mix flour, salt, pepper, and seafood seasoning and spread onto a large sheet of waxed paper. Dredge each medallion in flour, re-dip in egg wash, and dredge in flour once more. Place medallions in hot oil and fry until golden. Drain oil from medallions on a paper towel.

SERVES 4 to 6.

SIDE DISH SUGGESTIONS: Sautéed zucchini and crusty French bread.

GRILLED LEMON-BUTTER MACKEREL

Fresh mackerel, due to its very high oil content is extremely rich in omega-3 fatty acids. It is an excellent food for helping to lower cholesterol.

2 to 4 whole mackerel
½ cup butter
2 tablespoon lemon-pepper seasoning

When you purchase whole mackerel, ask the salesperson to remove the heads and to butterfly fish. (You may prefer to buy mackerel fillets.)

Place a non-stick fish tray or double sheet of aluminum foil on the grill rack and pre-heat the grill. Melt butter in the microwave or a saucepan. Add lemon-pepper seasoning and mix well. Brush lemon-butter over the skin side of each fish and place skin-side down on hot grill. Baste top of each fish with lemon-butter and cook until meat turns white. Use a spatula to remove fish from grill when cooked. Mackerel meat is very soft, so be very careful when handling cooked fish.

SERVES 2 to 4.

SIDE DISH SUGGESTIONS: Fresh cucumber salad and crusty bread.

DEEP-FRIED SMELTS

2 pounds whole, headless smelts
2 cups vegetable oil
2 eggs
¼ cup milk
1½ cups flour
2 tablespoons cornmeal
1 teaspoon salt
1 teaspoon pepper
2 tablespoons hot sauce

Pre-heat oil in a skillet at medium heat. Beat eggs and milk in a shallow bowl. Place smelts in egg wash for 1 minute. Mix flour, cornmeal, salt, and pepper and spread onto large sheet of waxed paper. Dredge each smelt in seasoned flour. Immediately drop smelts into hot oil and fry until golden brown. Drain excess oil by placing cooked smelts on a paper towel.

Note: Smelts, much like sardines, have small, soft bones that can be eaten and easily digested. Fried smelts can be enjoyed on a sandwich with hot sauce to taste.

SERVES 4 to 6.

SIDE DISH SUGGESTIONS: Celery sticks, sliced dill pickles, and potato chips.

STEAMED MONKFISH (Poor Man's Lobster)

Monkfish is also called the anglerfish. On the top of its head is an appendage that functions something like a fishing pole. The monkfish sits deep in the sand at the bottom of the ocean and dangles this lure in front of lobsters, crabs, and fish, attacking when they are within reach. Since the monkfish diet is primarily lobster, shrimp, crab, and scallops, the meat tends to be sweet like that of lobster. Hence its nickname: the "poor man's lobster." Once considered valueless, monkfish has become so popular over the past 10 years that it can hardly be called a "poor man's" meal anymore.

    1½ pounds monkfish tails
    2 cups water
    3 tablespoons vinegar
    1 cup butter

Add water and vinegar to a soup pot. Place a colander inside the pot. Turn heat to high. Slice monkfish tails into thin pieces. Layer the strips around the colander, cover the pot, and steam for 10 minutes. In a microwave or saucepan, melt butter. When monkfish is cooked, remove from heat and serve with hot butter.

SERVES 2 to 4.

SIDE DISH SUGGESTIONS: Baked potato and broccoli.

Monkfish

CURRIED ORANGE ROUGHY
WITH YELLOW RICE AND SNOW PEAS

    1 pound orange roughy fillets
    1 cup of yellow (flavored) rice
    1 6-ounce package frozen snow peas
    vegetable spray
    1 stick butter
    ¼ cup flour
    1 cup milk
    2½ tablespoons curry powder
    1 teaspoon salt
    1 teaspoon pepper

Cook rice according to instructions on package. Thaw snow peas and layer across the rice during last 2 minutes of cooking.

Pre-heat the oven to 400 degrees F. Spray baking dish with vegetable spray. Place fillets in single layer in the dish and bake for 5 minutes.

In a saucepan, melt butter. Add flour slowly, stirring until bubbly. Pour in milk slowly, stirring until sauce thickens. Add curry, salt, and pepper. Stir snow peas into rice and arrange around a large serving dish. Place orange roughy fillets over rice and spoon curry sauce onto each fillet.

SERVES 2 to 4.

SIDE DISH SUGGESTION: Fresh cucumber salad.

BROILED ORANGE ROUGHY WITH EGG SAUCE

    1 pound orange roughy fillets
    ½ cup water
    1 fish bouillon cube
    4 tablespoons butter
    2 tablespoons cornstarch
    1 hard-boiled egg, finely diced
    ½ teaspoon salt
    vegetable spray

Pre-heat the broiler. Add ¼ cup water, fish bouillon, and butter to a medium saucepan at low heat. Melt butter and press bouillon with a fork to dissolve. Mix cornstarch and remaining water in a cup until creamy and add to the butter mixture. Stir until sauce thickens. Add salt and eggs and stir gently.

Spray broiler pan with vegetable spray and place fillets on pan. Spoon a thin layer of egg sauce on each fillet and broil about 4 inches from heat until center of fish is flaky when cut with a fork. Remove fish from heat, place each portion on a serving dish and add remaining egg sauce to top of each fillet.

SERVES 2 to 4.

SIDE DISH SUGGESTIONS: Chopped spinach and mashed potatoes.

BROILED ORANGE ROUGHY VEGGIE MEDLEY

1 pound orange roughy fillets
1 yellow squash
1 red or yellow bell pepper
1 stalk broccoli
4 ounces sliced almonds
4 tablespoons butter, melted
2 teaspoons lemon-pepper seasoning

Pre-heat the oven to 425 degrees F. Slice squash and bell pepper into thin strips. Discard stem from broccoli and cut remainder into florets. Place 2 tablespoons butter in a saucepan and add vegetables. Sauté at low heat just until vegetable colors become bright—they should not be fully cooked. Pour butter-vegetable mixture into a baking dish. Layer vegetables across bottom of dish and layer fish fillets on top. Cover top of fillets with sliced almonds and sprinkles of lemon-pepper seasoning. Drizzle with the remaining melted butter.

Bake for 15 minutes. Check center of a fillet with a fork to see that it flakes and is white in center.

SERVES 2 to 4.

SIDE DISH SUGGESTIONS: Spinach salad and cottage cheese.

BAKED OCEAN PERCH FILLETS
WITH MUSHROOM SAUCE

 1½ pounds ocean perch fillets
 ½ cup fresh mushrooms, chopped
 2 scallions, chopped
 ¼ cup butter
 1 teaspoon salt
 1 teaspoon pepper
 1 tablespoon flour
 ¼ cup heavy cream

Pre-heat the oven to 425 degrees F. In a small saucepan, melt butter. Stir in mushrooms, scallions, salt, and pepper and cook at low heat until scallions soften. Stir in flour and slowly add cream, stirring until sauce thickens.

Place perch fillets in a baking pan. Cover each fillet with mushroom sauce and bake for 15 minutes. Check center of a fillet with a fork. Meat, when cooked perfectly, will be flaky and white. Remove fish to serving plates, stir up sauce remaining in baking pan, and serve over fillets.

SERVES 2 to 4.

SIDE DISH SUGGESTIONS: Wild rice and steamed zucchini.

CAMPFIRE BROOK OR RAINBOW TROUT COOKOUT

 2 pounds brook or rainbow trout fillets, skin-on
 aluminum foil
 1 medium onion
 2 stalks of celery
 2 carrots, peeled
 2 medium potatoes
 1 teaspoon garlic, crushed or chopped
 1 14½-ounce can diced tomatoes
 1 teaspoon salt
 1 teaspoon pepper
 ½ cup margarine

Build a campfire in contained, safe area using kindling and small logs. Place a metal grate over flames. Allow the fire to burn down to hot embers. Cut a 3-foot length of foil and fold in half. Draw edges upward to form a bowl shape. Slice onion, celery, carrots, and potatoes no more than ¼-inch thick. Place fish in foil; add sliced vegetables, garlic, tomatoes, salt, pepper, and margarine. Fold edges tightly to form a cooking pouch. Poke two small holes in top of pouch for steam vents. Place the foil cooking pouch on the hot metal grate and cook for 20 minutes. Remove from heat and open carefully. Contents will be hot and steamy. Serve fish on plate with vegetables and cooking juices.

SERVES 4 to 6.

SIDE DISH SUGGESTIONS: Tossed salad and crusty buttered bread.

TROUT NANETTE

2 to 4 whole rainbow trout, cleaned and gutted
1 cup long grain wild rice
3 tablespoons butter
1 small onion, chopped
1 clove garlic, finely chopped
1 cup mushrooms, sliced thin
3 tablespoons cooking sherry
½ can cream of mushroom soup
1 egg
1 slice bread
vegetable spray

Pre-heat the oven to 425 degrees F. Cook wild rice according to instructions on the package. In a saucepan, melt butter at low heat and sauté onion, garlic, and mushrooms until soft. Add sherry and cream of mushroom soup and simmer for 2 minutes. Remove sauté from stove and mix in one beaten egg, crumbled bread, and rice.

Rinse the belly of the trout under cold running water. Stuff belly cavity with a generous amount of mushroom/rice stuffing. Spray a baking dish with vegetable spray and place stuffed trout in dish in a single layer. Spray tops of fish with vegetable spray and bake for 20 minutes. Check the center of a trout near the bone with a fork. Meat should be white and flaky.

SERVES 2 to 4.

SIDE DISH SUGGESTIONS: French style string beans and sourdough bread.

EVAN'S SAN FELIPE CHILEAN SEA BASS FILLETS

1½ pounds Chilean sea bass fillets
1 clove garlic, finely chopped
2 tablespoons butter
2 tablespoons flour
¼ cup orange juice
¼ cup milk
¼ cup fresh cilantro, chopped
2 tablespoons flour
1 teaspoon chili powder

Melt butter in a large skillet and sauté garlic at medium heat. Cut fillets in half and sauté them in garlic-butter until meat turns white and flaky, about 3 to 5 minutes. Remove fish from skillet, leaving remaining butter/garlic mixture. Reduce heat to low, stir in flour, and cook until bubbly. Slowly add orange juice and milk, stirring until sauce thickens. Remove the sauce from heat; sprinkle in chopped cilantro and chili powder. Mix well and serve sauce over fish.

SERVES 4 to 6.

SIDE DISH SUGGESTIONS: Sliced avocado and pita bread wedges.

CHILEAN SEA BASS MARSEILLAISE

1½ to 2 pounds sea bass fillets
½ teaspoon salt
½ teaspoon pepper
3 tablespoons olive oil
1 medium onion, chopped
1 clove garlic, minced
2 tablespoons parsley, chopped
½ cup dry white wine
1 14½-can diced tomatoes
1 tablespoon flour

Cut fillet into serving portions (4 to 6 ounces). Sprinkle each with salt and pepper. Heat oil in a large skillet at medium heat. Add fillets and cook until firm and flaky at center. Remove fish from pan and set aside. Reduce heat to low and add chopped onion, garlic, and parsley. Sauté for 2 minutes. Stir in flour and cook until bubbly. Add wine and tomatoes, and stir until sauce thickens.

Remove skillet from heat. Return fish to skillet and cover with sauce. Allow one minute before serving. Place fillets on serving dishes and spoon sauce on each.

SERVES 4 to 6.

SIDE DISH SUGGESTIONS: Fresh snap beans and rice pilaf.

SWEET AND SOUR SEA BASS WITH CASHEWS

1 pound sea bass fillets
1 cup oil
1 cup flour
1 teaspoon salt
1 teaspoon pepper
1 egg
½ cup milk
Sweet and sour sauce
2 tablespoons pineapple juice
1 tablespoon brown sugar
1 teaspoon lemon juice
1 tablespoon ketchup
1 teaspoon soy sauce
½ teaspoon vinegar
½ cup whole raw unsalted cashew nuts
1 tablespoon cornstarch
¼ cup water

In a saucepan, mix all ingredients for sweet and sour sauce (except cornstarch and water). Simmer at low heat for 2 minutes, then set aside to cool.

Pre-heat oil at medium/high heat in a wok or large skillet. Cut fillets into serving portions about 3 inches each. Mix flour, salt, and pepper and spread onto a large sheet of waxed paper. Beat egg and milk in a bowl, and dip each fillet into egg wash. Dredge each fillet in the flour; fry until golden. Remove from heat and lay fillets on paper towel to drain excess oil. Discard oil from skillet, leaving just a thin coating. Return skillet to heat and stir-fry cashew nuts for 3 minutes.

Return sweet and sour sauce to low heat. When it begins to bubble, mix cornstarch in a cup with water until creamy and slowly add it to the sauce, stirring until sauce thickens. Place fillets on a serving dish and pour sauce over each. Garnish with roasted cashew nuts.

SERVES 2 to 4.

SIDE DISH SUGGESTION: Tossed salad.

WHITING IN SHERRY SOUR CREAM SAUCE

Whiting fillets usually are sold frozen, skin on. Most are from Argentina.

2 pounds boneless whiting fillets
3 tablespoons butter or margarine
2 tablespoons cooking sherry
1 medium onion, minced
1 tablespoon Dijon mustard
1 cup sour cream
1 teaspoon salt
1 teaspoon coarse black pepper
vegetable spray
½ teaspoon paprika
1 teaspoon chives, finely chopped
2 lemons

If frozen, thaw whiting overnight in refrigerator. Pre-heat broiler. Melt butter or margarine with sherry in a saucepan at low heat; add onion and sauté until soft. Remove from heat and stir in mustard and sour cream. Sprinkle salt and pepper on each fillet. Spray broiler tray with vegetable oil and place fillets in a single layer on tray. Broil for 5 to 7 minutes. Check fillets by flaking center with a fork. When cooked properly, remove from oven and arrange on a serving plate. Spoon sour cream sauce over fillets. Garnish with paprika and chopped chives. Circle edge of dish with thin slices of lemon.

SERVES 4 to 6.

SIDE DISH SUGGESTIONS: Cornbread and creamed spinach.

BUTTERFLY DEEP SOUTH-FRIED WHITING SANDWICH

4 pounds frozen whiting, headless and gutted
3 cups oil
3 eggs
½ cup milk
1 cup flour
3 cups cornmeal
1 tablespoon salt
1 tablespoon seafood seasoning or Old Bay Seasoning
Louisiana hot sauce to taste
Sliced bread

Thaw whiting under cold running water or overnight in refrigerator. With a sharp knife slice through bottom of the fish to the backbone.

Run the point of the knife along each side of the bone until it reaches the top of the fish. (Do not cut through the skin on top.) Take a paper towel and grab the head side of the backbone and gently pull up and to the tail to remove the backbone in one piece.

Use fingers to feel for small bones along belly, and remove them with the edge of the knife. Open the fish to make a butterfly shape.

Pre-heat the oil in a deep skillet (preferably cast iron) at medium/high heat. Beat eggs and milk. Blend flour, cornmeal, salt, and seafood seasoning and spread onto a large sheet of waxed paper. Dip each butterfly whiting into the egg wash and then into the flour mix. Drop each into hot oil and fry until golden. Drain excess oil from fish on paper towels. Serve on sandwich bread with hot sauce.

SERVES 4 to 6.

SIDE DISH SUGGESTIONS: Hush puppies and cole slaw.

GRILLED MIAMI BEACH KINGFISH STEAKS WITH CUCUMBER SAUCE

1½ pounds kingfish steaks, ½ inch thick
1 teaspoon salt
1 teaspoon pepper
1 teaspoon paprika
vegetable spray
½ cup fresh cucumber, peeled and coarsely chopped
½ teaspoon fresh dill, chopped
¼ cup mayonnaise
½ teaspoon lemon juice
2 whole fresh tomatoes

Pre-heat the grill. Mix salt, pepper, and paprika and sprinkle generously on each steak. Spray grill with vegetable spray and place steaks on rack. Grill both sides for about 3 minutes.

Combine cucumber, dill, mayonnaise, and lemon juice in a blender or food processor and puree. Cut fresh tomatoes in half and with a spoon scoop out the centers.

When fish steaks are cooked, remove from grill. Place a portion on each serving plate. Spoon cucumber sauce into each tomato and arrange alongside cooked fish.

SERVES 2 to 4.

SIDE DISH SUGGESTIONS: Garlic bread, sautéed plantains, and black beans.

SOUTH-OF-THE-BORDER SNAPPER TORTILLA WRAP

1½ pounds snapper fillets
2 cups olive oil
1 medium onion, chopped
1 green bell pepper, chopped
1 small fresh jalapeño chile, chopped
2 fresh tomatoes, chopped
1 teaspoon garlic, crushed or minced
1 egg
¼ cup milk
2 cups flour
1 tablespoon chili powder
1 teaspoon salt
6 to 10 flour tortillas
½ cup shredded cheddar cheese

In a saucepan, heat 2 tablespoons oil and sauté onion, bell pepper, jalapeño, and tomatoes with garlic at low heat. Remove from heat and set aside.

Pre-heat oil in a skillet at medium heat. Wrap tortillas in foil and warm in oven at 375 degrees F for 10 to 15 minutes. In a bowl beat egg and milk. Mix flour with chili powder and salt and spread onto a large sheet of waxed paper. Cut fillets into strips and dip in egg wash. Dredge each in flour, and fry until golden. Place fillets on steamed flour tortillas and add sauce as desired. Sprinkle cheese over sauce to taste. Wrap tortilla around the food and eat.

SERVES 4 to 6.

SIDE DISH SUGGESTIONS: Celery sticks and imported Greek salad peppers.

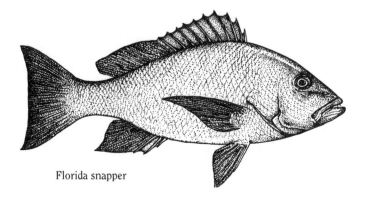

Florida snapper

TERESA'S TERRIFIC "TAILGATE PARTY" TURBOT

2 pounds turbot fillets
2 tablespoon olive oil
1 clove garlic, minced
1 yellow or red bell pepper, sliced
½ bunch fresh scallions, chopped
1 peeled carrot, chopped
½ teaspoon vinegar
½ teaspoon soy sauce
2 tablespoons dry white wine
aluminum foil
½ cup butter
1 teaspoon salt
¼ cup water

On the night before or morning of the "big game," chop vegetables, heat oil in a saucepan at low heat, and sauté vegetables until soft. Mix vinegar, water, soy sauce, and wine and pour into saucepan with veggies. Cook for one minute. Remove vegetables and juices from heat and allow mixture to cool. Transfer to a plastic container and seal with a lid. Refrigerate until ready to use.

At the tailgate party, pre-heat the grill or hibachi. Line the grilling grate with a double layer of aluminum foil and curl up edges ½ inch to form a tray. Melt butter on grill, place fillets on grill, sprinkle each with salt and cook for 2 minutes. (Do not turn the fish.) Pour sauce onto fish and cook for 3 to 5 minutes. Flake the center of a fillet with a fork to be sure it is cooked. Place turbot on a hard roll, spoon vegetables and juices over fish, and enjoy the party.

SERVES 4 to 6.

SIDE DISH SUGGESTIONS: Potato chips and sweet pickles.

GULF COAST FARM SEAFOOD

CATFISH, TILAPIA, HYBRID STRIPED BASS, AND CRAWFISH

The greatest successes in farm raising seafood in the United States have been achieved with catfish, tilapia, hybrid striped bass, and crawfish. In the Gulf states, hundreds of fish farms dot the coast.

Catfish farming began around 1960 in the Mississippi Delta. Today, farm-raised catfish is a big crop responsible for millions of dollars in annual revenue for Mississippi, Arkansas, Alabama, and Georgia. Catfish ranks fifth on the list of most-consumed fish in America.

Tilapia, which was introduced in America in the 1960s, originated in the Nile River. Often referred to as "Saint Peter's Fish," it gets this name from the belief that this species may have been the fish offered by Jesus to feed the masses. Tilapia has a mild, sweet flavor.

Hybrid striped bass is a genetically engineered fish that was designed to substitute for wild striped bass. Wild striped bass has always been considered the finest tasting fish. When it became endangered because of various environmental threats, many states restricted catch or enacted stringent size requirements to help the fish rebound.

Striped bass

The hybrid, a cross between wild striped bass and white bass, has an excellent flavor and is now much in demand at "white tablecloth" restaurants in New York, Los Angeles, Chicago, and other cities.

Crawfish is another favorite southern aquatic species. Farmed and growing wild beneath the surface of the many rice paddies of Louisiana, these miniature lobster-like creatures are traditionally used in Creole and Cajun cooking. They are prized for their sweet tender taste and most famous for their contribution to jambalaya, bisque, and etouffée.

Cooking caution: Be extremely careful when working with Cajun or any other hot seasoning. Avoid any contact with the eyes while handling of this type of spice—it may cause severe eye irritation. The hands should be washed immediately after handling it.

BLACKENED CATFISH FILLETS

1½ pounds catfish fillets
2 tablespoons oil
½ cup water
3 tablespoons blackening or Cajun seasoning, or
　　homemade mixture:
　　　1 teaspoon each of garlic and onion powders, paprika,
　　　ground red pepper, white pepper, black pepper;
　　　½ teaspoon each of dried ground thyme, oregano, bay leaf
2 teaspoons salt
1 fresh lemon

Note: Blackened dishes produce smoke when cooking. Be sure to cook under an exhaust fan, and keep room well vented.

　　Pre-heat oil in an iron skillet at high heat. (The pan must be very hot to cook this dish properly and quickly.) Dip catfish in water. Mix spices or spread blackening seasoning on a plate. Place each fillet on spice and press gently with hand to coat fish. Turn and coat opposite side. Place all fillets in hot skillet. Cook each side until seasoning turns "coal" black. This will produce some smoke. The fish will not burn. The blackening acts as a buffer and locks moisture in the fish. Once both sides of the fish are well blackened, remove fish from heat, squeeze lemon over each fillet and serve.

SERVES 2 to 4.

SIDE DISH SUGGESTIONS: Applesauce and cornbread.

LOUISIANA STYLE FRIED CATFISH

4 to 6 medium whole catfish, headless and skinless
2 eggs
¼ cup milk
2 cups cornmeal
½ cup flour
2 cups vegetable oil
1 teaspoon salt
1 teaspoon cayenne pepper
3 tablespoons hot sauce

Beat eggs with milk in a large, shallow mixing bowl. Blend cornmeal, flour, salt, and pepper on a large sheet of waxed paper. Pre-heat the oil in a deep skillet (preferably cast iron) at medium/high heat, 350 degrees F. Dip catfish in egg wash and dredge in flour mix. Dip a second time in egg wash and dredge again in flour mix. Fry in hot oil until batter turns brown and crispy. Check center of one fish by flaking with a fork to be sure fish is cooked. Catfish meat turns white when cooked.

Remove fish from the heat and drain excess oil by placing fish in colander or on a paper towel. Place fish on serving plates and drizzle with hot sauce to desired taste.

SERVES 4 to 6.

SIDE DISH SUGGESTIONS: Hush puppies and coleslaw.

BROILED CAJUN CATFISH FILLETS

2 pounds catfish fillets
2 tablespoons margarine
3 tablespoons Cajun seasoning
2 tablespoons water
½ bunch fresh scallions, chopped
1 fresh carrot, shredded
vegetable spray

Melt margarine and mix with Cajun seasoning, water, scallions, and shredded carrot in a large bowl. Place catfish in the bowl and allow the fish to marinate in refrigerator for at least one hour.

Pre-heat the broiler. Spray the broiler tray with vegetable spray. Place catfish fillets on tray and drizzle with marinade. Broil the fish for 7 to 10 minutes. While fish is cooking, pour remaining marinade in a small saucepan and simmer on low heat. Check fish after 7 minutes by flaking center with a fork to be sure fish is cooked. Remove fillets from oven and place on serving dishes. Spoon remaining marinade over each fillet. SERVES 4 to 6.

SIDE DISH SUGGESTIONS: Sautéed okra and hot rolls.

PINEAPPLE BBQ GRILLED CATFISH AND VEGETABLE MEDLEY

1½ pounds catfish fillets
½ cup ketchup
1 teaspoon brown sugar
¼ cup vinegar
1 tablespoon chili powder
1 small can crushed pineapple
¼ cup water
1 teaspoon salt
aluminum foil
2 potatoes, diced small
1 onion, minced
1 green bell pepper, sliced

Pre-heat the grill. In a large bowl, mix ketchup, sugar, vinegar, chili powder, crushed pineapple, water, and salt. Cut catfish fillets in half and place in marinade for 5 minutes.

Cut a 3-foot piece of aluminum foil. Fold the foil in half and curl up edges to form a bowl. Place catfish and sliced vegetables in the foil. Cover with marinade and then close foil to form a tight cooking pouch. Poke two holes in top of foil for heat vents and place the meal on the grill. Cover the grill and cook for 20 minutes.

SERVES 2 to 4.

SIDE DISH SUGGESTIONS: Celery sticks and crusty bread.

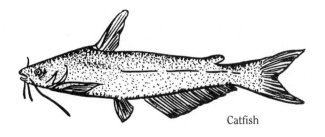

Catfish

BROILED LEMON-PEPPER CATFISH FILLETS

1½ pounds catfish fillets
2 tablespoons butter
2 tablespoons lemon-pepper seasoning
vegetable spray

Pre-heat the broiler. Mix melted butter and lemon-pepper seasoning in a shallow bowl. Place fish fillets in seasoning; mix gently to coat both sides of fish. Spray broiler tray with vegetable spray and place fillets on tray. Broil for 6 minutes. Brush remaining butter and lemon-pepper sauce over fish and cook for 2 more minutes. Remove from heat and serve.

SERVES 4 to 6.

SIDE DISH SUGGESTIONS: Carrots and baked potato.

QUICK DINNER CURRY CATFISH NUGGETS

2 pounds catfish nuggets
2 cups yellow (flavored) rice
3 tablespoons vegetable oil
½ cup onion, finely chopped
1 can cream of mushroom soup
¼ cup milk
1 cup frozen sweet peas
1½ teaspoons curry powder

Catfish nuggets are small wedges of meat cut from near the belly of the fish. Many stores sell these, fresh or frozen, at a very good price. You can also cut fillets into cubes to make nuggets, although the taste may be slightly different.

Cook rice according to instructions on package. Pre-heat the oil at medium/high heat in a large skillet. Sauté chopped onion and catfish nuggets in oil until onions are soft and fish is cooked. Reduce heat to low and add cream of mushroom soup, milk, peas, and curry powder. Simmer for 2 minutes. Place rice on a large serving dish and cover with catfish nuggets and sauce.

SERVES 4 to 6.

SIDE DISH SUGGESTIONS: Tossed salad and cottage cheese.

EASY TILAPIA SAUTÉ

1 pound tilapia fillets
1 tablespoon olive oil
1 clove garlic, finely chopped
2 tablespoons milk
3 tablespoons butter
1 cup fresh mushrooms, sliced

Pre-heat skillet at medium heat. Sauté garlic in oil until toasted. Sauté mushrooms until done and remove from pan. Place fillets in pan and cook each side for 4 minutes. Flake center of fillet with a fork to check for full cooking. Remove fillets from pan and place on serving dishes. Reduce heat to low. Add mushrooms, milk, and butter to pan and stir until hot. Spoon butter/mushroom sauce over each fillet and serve.
SERVES 2 to 3.
SIDE DISH SUGGESTIONS: French style string beans and boiled parsley potatoes.

BAKED STRIPED BASS STUFFED WITH CRABMEAT

3 to 4 small whole hybrid (or wild) striped bass
½ pound crabmeat
¼ cup celery, chopped
¼ cup onion, chopped
1 egg
3 tablespoons mayonnaise
¼ teaspoon mustard
¼ teaspoon seafood seasoning
2 tablespoons butter
1 slice of bread, crumbled
vegetable spray

Melt butter in a skillet, add celery and onion and cook until soft. In a bowl, mix egg, mayonnaise, mustard, seafood seasoning, crabmeat, celery, onion, and crumbled bread. Pre-heat the oven to 350 degrees F. Rinse belly of fish under cold running water. Fill the clean belly cavity of the fish with stuffing. Spray a baking dish with vegetable spray; place fish in a dish and bake for about 20 minutes. Check stuffing by removing a sample with a fork. (Stuffing needs to be hot enough so that egg is cooked.) Flake the meat of the fish with a fork down to the bone to see whether it is fully cooked. Add additional cooking time in 2-minute increments as needed.
SERVES 2 to 4.
SIDE DISH SUGGESTION: Potatoes and asparagus.

"BIG EASY" CRAWFISH, MICROWAVED OR STEAMED

   3 pounds whole cooked crawfish
   2 tablespoons Cajun seasoning
   2 cups water
   2 tablespoons vinegar

Note: In most parts of the country (except Louisiana) crawfish is sold cooked. Therefore, when preparing crawfish for a "pick and eat" meal, you only need to heat and serve the crawfish. As an option, you can also enjoy the crawfish as a cold dish.

To microwave: Place the crawfish on a large serving plate. Sprinkle generous amounts of Cajun seasoning over the crawfish. Microwave on high for 1½ minutes. Serve hot. Pick meat from tails and sip the juice from the heads. (Be careful with Cajun seasoning to avoid contact with eyes. Wash hands immediately after eating and handling seasoning.)

To steam: Pour 2 cups of water and 2 tablespoons of vinegar in deep pot. Set a colander inside pot. Place a layer of crawfish in the colander; sprinkle with Cajun seasoning, adding layers until colander is full. Bring water to boil at high heat, cover the pot, and steam for 2 minutes. Serve crawfish hot. Pick meat from tails and sip juice from the heads.

SERVES 4 to 6.

SIDE DISH SUGGESTION: Corn on the cob.

CRAWFISH ETOUFFÉE

   1½ pounds crawfish tails
   ½ cup butter
   1 large onion, minced
   1 tablespoon garlic, crushed or minced
   1 sweet green pepper, minced
   ½ teaspoon salt
   ½ teaspoon pepper
   ¼ teaspoon Cajun seasoning
   ½ fresh lemon

Melt butter in a medium-sized skillet at medium heat. Sauté onions, garlic, and peppers until soft. Add crawfish tails, sprinkle with salt, pepper, and Cajun seasoning. Simmer for 10 minutes. Squeeze lemon over etouffée just before serving.

SERVES 4 TO 6.

SIDE DISH SUGGESTIONS: Hot biscuits and steamed zucchini.

XIV

SOUPS, CHOWDERS, AND BISQUES

THREE-STEP BEST DARN CHUNKY SHRIMP BISQUE
(Thaw, Chop, Stir)

> 1 pound bag raw frozen salad shrimp, peeled and deveined
> 2 tablespoons butter
> ½ bunch fresh scallions
> 2 peeled potatoes
> 2 peeled carrots
> 1 quart half-and-half
> ¼ teaspoon salt
> ¼ teaspoon Old Bay Seasoning or seafood seasoning
> 2 tablespoons flour
> ½ cup water

Thaw salad shrimp and rinse. **Chop** scallions fine and dice potatoes and carrots. Cook vegetables in boiling water until soft. Drain water. Using a 1-quart pot, add butter and place on medium heat. Add half-and-half, vegetables, shrimp, salt, and Old Bay Seasoning to pot. **Stir.** Reduce liquid by ¼ at medium heat, with constant stirring. Once bisque has reached a boil, reduce heat to low. Whisk flour and water in a cup until creamy, then pour into bisque and stir to thicken. Remove from heat and serve hot.

SERVES 4 to 5.

SIDE DISH SUGGESTIONS: Hot biscuits and fresh cucumber slices.

HEARTY CRAB BISQUE

1 pound special blue crabmeat or Dungeness crabmeat
2 tablespoons butter
½ bunch fresh scallions, finely chopped
1 quart half-and-half
¼ teaspoon salt
¼ teaspoon Old Bay Seasoning or seafood seasoning
2 teaspoons flour
½ cup water

Place butter in a 1-quart pot over medium heat. Add scallions and cook until soft. Add half-and-half, crabmeat, salt, and Old Bay Seasoning to pot and stir. Reduce liquid by ¼ at medium heat, with constant stirring. Once bisque has reached a boil, reduce heat to low. Whisk flour and water in a cup until creamy, then pour into bisque and stir to thicken. Remove from heat and serve hot.

SERVES 4 to 5.

SIDE DISH SUGGESTION: Grilled cheese sandwiches.

MARYLAND STYLE CRAB SOUP

1 pound cooked crabmeat, any type
2 15-ounce cans peeled baby carrots
2 15-ounce cans peeled whole potatoes
1 14½-ounce can whole string beans
1 cup celery, coarsely chopped
½ cup onion, coarsely chopped
1 1-pound can of crushed tomatoes
3 quarts water
4 beef bouillon cubes
½ teaspoon salt
4 tablespoons Old Bay Seasoning (more for hotter taste)

Cut carrots and potatoes in half. In a large soup stockpot add halved vegetables, whole string beans, celery, onions, tomatoes, crabmeat, water, bouillon, and seasonings. Place on high heat, bring to a boil, and then reduce heat to simmer for 30 minutes.

Option: Use equivalent amounts of raw carrots, potatoes, and string beans.

SERVES 4 to 6.

SIDE DISH SUGGESTION: Crusty bread and butter.

LOBSTER CHOWDER

New Englanders make two meals from a lobster. Chowder is especially good the day after a big lobster meal. Cook one extra lobster and save it for the chowder.

6 ounces cooked lobster meat
2 tablespoons butter
½ bunch fresh scallions, finely chopped
2 peeled potatoes
2 peeled carrots (optional)
1 quart half-and-half
¼ teaspoon salt
¼ teaspoon seafood seasoning
2 tablespoons flour
½ cup water

Pick cooked lobster meat. Dice potatoes and carrots and cook in boiling water until soft. Melt butter in a one-quart pot over medium heat. Add scallions and cook until soft. Add half-and-half, vegetables, lobster meat, salt, and seafood seasoning to pot and stir. Reduce liquid by ¼ at medium heat, with constant stirring. Once chowder has reached a boil, reduce heat to low. Whisk flour and water in a cup until creamy, then pour into chowder and stir to thicken. Remove from heat and serve hot.
SERVES 4.
SIDE DISH SUGGESTION: Buttered biscuits.

MANHATTAN CLAM CHOWDER

2 dozen large raw clams, shucked
1 cup celery, coarsely chopped
¼ cup onion, coarsely chopped
2 potatoes, peeled and diced
½ teaspoon salt and pepper
1 1-pound can crushed tomatoes
3 quarts water
1 teaspoon thyme

Rinse clams and chop them fine. Add all ingredients to a large soup stockpot and place on high heat. Bring to a boil, reduce heat, and simmer for 30 minutes.
SERVES 4 to 6.
SIDE DISH SUGGESTION: Hot dinner rolls with honey butter.

NEW ENGLAND CLAM CHOWDER

1 pint raw shucked clams
2 tablespoons butter
½ bunch fresh scallions, finely chopped
2 stalks celery, finely chopped
1 quart half-and-half
2 potatoes, peeled and diced
2 slices crisp bacon, crumbled
¼ teaspoon salt
¼ teaspoon pepper
2 tablespoons flour
½ cup water

Chop the clams into four pieces and save juice. Select a 2-quart saucepan; add butter and place on medium heat. Cook scallions and celery until bright green and soft. Add half-and-half, potatoes, clams (including juice), bacon, salt, and pepper and stir. Reduce liquid by ¼ at medium heat, stirring constantly. Reduce heat to low. Whisk flour and water in a cup until creamy, then pour into chowder and stir to thicken. Remove from heat and serve hot.
SERVES 4.
SIDE DISH SUGGESTIONS: Tossed salad and bread sticks.

OYSTER STEW

1 pint shucked oysters, any size, any species
¼ cup margarine or butter
1 quart half-and-half
¼ teaspoon salt
¼ teaspoon pepper
2 drops Tabasco sauce
1 teaspoon dry parsley
1 teaspoon paprika

Reserve juice from oysters. Melt margarine in a 2-quart saucepan at medium heat. Pour in half-and-half, add salt and pepper, and stir constantly until stew begins to bubble. Add oysters (including juice) and cook just until the oysters' edges curl. Add Tabasco sauce. Spoon stew into bowls and garnish with parsley and paprika.
SERVES 4 to 6.
SIDE DISH SUGGESTIONS: Oyster crackers and sliced cheese.

CRAWFISH BISQUE

8 ounces crawfish tail meat
2 tablespoons butter
½ bunch scallions, coarsely chopped
1 quart half-and-half
1 teaspoon salt
1 teaspoon pepper
1 teaspoon parsley
½ cup water
2 tablespoons flour

Chop crawfish tails into coarse pieces. Melt butter in a saucepan at medium heat and sauté scallions until soft. Reduce heat to low. Add half-and-half, salt, pepper, and parsley. Stir constantly until bisque begins to bubble. Mix flour and water. Pour into bisque and stir until it thickens. Mix in crawfish and cook for one minute. Remove from heat and serve.
SERVES 4 to 6.
SIDE DISH SUGGESTION: Crusty bread.

GLOUCESTER FISH CHOWDER

1 pound cod fillets
½ cup butter
½ teaspoon salt
½ teaspoon black pepper
½ cup water
4 fish bouillon cubes
3 scallions, coarsely chopped
1 quart half-and-half
1 medium potato, peeled and diced
2 tablespoons flour

Cut fish into small pieces. In a medium-sized soup pot, melt butter; add salt, pepper, ¼ cup of water, and bouillon cubes and cook at medium heat. Stir in chopped scallions and fish. When bouillon cubes are dissolved and fish is white, add half-and-half and potatoes. Cook until liquid reduces by ¼. Mix flour with ¼ cup of water and stir into chowder until it thickens. Continue cooking on low heat for 5 minutes.
SERVES 2 to 4.
SIDE DISH SUGGESTIONS: Hot freshly baked bread and salad.

FISHERMAN'S STEW

1 pound mild fish fillets (flounder, snapper, cod, or haddock)
½ cup olive oil
1 teaspoon garlic, crushed or minced
½ pound mushrooms, sliced
¼ teaspoon fennel seed, crushed
½ teaspoon celery seed
½ teaspoon salt
½ teaspoon black pepper
4 fish bouillon cubes
4½ cups water
3 potatoes, diced and peeled
1 cup frozen corn
1 cup whole frozen baby carrots
1 16-ounce can tomato puree
3 tablespoons flour

Cut fish into bite-sized cubes. Pre-heat deep skillet at medium-high heat, add oil, fish, garlic, mushrooms, fennel seed, celery seed, salt and pepper and cook until fish is white throughout. Add fish bouillon and 4 cups of water. Reduce heat to low. Add vegetables and tomato puree to fish stew. Simmer for 20 minutes. Mix flour with water, stir into stew to thicken, and continue to simmer for 3 minutes. Remove from heat and serve.

SERVES 4 to 6.

SIDE DISH SUGGESTION: Hot buttered biscuits.

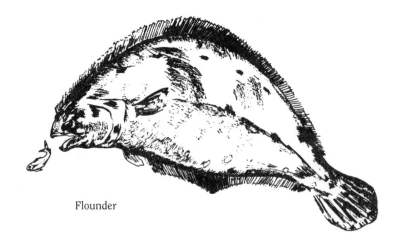

Flounder

FISH AND CORN CHOWDER

1 pound flounder, cod, haddock, or turbot fillets
2 cups water
2 small potatoes, peeled and diced
1½ cups frozen corn
1 small onion, finely chopped
1 quart whole milk
1 tablespoon butter
2 fish bouillon cubes
1 teaspoon Old Bay Seasoning or seafood seasoning
1 teaspoon salt
1 teaspoon pepper
2 tablespoons flour
¼ cup water

In a 2-quart pot boil water. Add potatoes, corn, and onion and cook until vegetables soften. Check fillets for bones and remove if found. Cut fish into ½-inch cubes. Drain vegetables and rinse under cold water. Wash and dry the pot. Pour in milk with butter and bouillon cubes. Place on medium heat and bring to a bubble. Add fish and stir gently for 5 minutes. Check a fish cube by cutting it in half. Center should be white and flaky. (Boiled fish cooks quickly. The key here is not to overcook.) Add seasoning, salt, pepper, and vegetables. Whisk flour and water until creamy. Pour into chowder and stir to thicken.
SERVES 4 TO 6.
SIDE DISH SUGGESTION: Hot biscuits.

See also: **Easy Captain's Catch Bouillabaisse,** page 157

SEAFOOD SALADS

"REAL" FRESH TUNA SALAD

If you have never tried fresh tuna salad, you owe yourself this treat. Canned tuna is overcooked to the point of tenderness and packed in oil or water. The tuna sits in the can for months and months. It tastes almost nothing like fresh tuna. You have not had a great tuna salad until you make your own "real" fresh tuna salad.

½ to ¾ pound fresh tuna
½ teaspoon lemon-pepper seasoning
3 stalks celery, finely chopped
½ onion (optional), finely chopped
¼ cup mayonnaise
white bread, toasted, or lettuce

Follow cooking instructions for **Perfect Baked Tuna** (Chapter 6). Place baked tuna in refrigerator overnight. The next day, in a large mixing bowl, break cold tuna into fingertip-sized chunks. Sprinkle with lemon-pepper seasoning. Add celery, onion, and mayonnaise, and mix gently. Serve on bed of crisp lettuce or on toasted white bread.

SERVES 4 to 6.

SIDE DISH SUGGESTIONS: Macaroni salad and sliced tomatoes.

FRESH TOMATOES STUFFED WITH TUNA SALAD

½ pound fresh tuna steak
2 tablespoons margarine
1 teaspoon pepper
½ teaspoon lemon juice
3 large fresh tomatoes
¼ cup mayonnaise
2 celery stalks, finely chopped
1 teaspoon pickle relish
¼ head iceberg lettuce, thinly shredded

Cut tuna into ¼- to ½-inch cubes. Heat margarine in a skillet at medium heat. Season tuna cubes with pepper and lemon. Sauté the cubes until they turn white. Remove from heat and chill in refrigerator for 1 hour.

Cut tops off the tomatoes. Slice a small piece from the bottom so that they will stand flat on serving dish. Use a spoon to scoop out the center of tomatoes.

Mix cold tuna cubes with mayonnaise, celery, and pickle relish. Place a layer of shredded lettuce in each tomato, allowing the lettuce to hang over the sides. Fill each tomato with fresh tuna salad. Serve cold.
SERVES 3.
SIDE DISH SUGGESTIONS: Fresh sliced radishes and assorted cheeses.

SHRIMP AND FRESH FRUIT SALAD

8 ounces cooked salad shrimp or cocktail shrimp
1 honeydew melon
1 kiwi
½ pint strawberries
½ pint blueberries
1 can mandarin orange slices

Cut melon in half. Scoop out fruit using a melon baller. Save emptied-out melon halves. Peel and slice kiwi. Remove stems from strawberries. Cut each berry in half the long way. Drain juice from oranges. Rinse blueberries in cold water. In a large mixing bowl, toss all ingredients except kiwi slices. Fill the cavity of each melon with fruit and shrimp mixture. Garnish top of salad with kiwi slices.
SERVES 4 to 6.
SERVE as an appetizer.

CLASSIC SHRIMP SALAD

 1 pound shell-on shrimp, 36/40 count or smaller
 2 stalks celery, finely chopped
 3 tablespoons regular or fat-free mayonnaise
 1 teaspoon lemon-pepper seasoning
 ½ teaspoon Old Bay Seasoning or seafood seasoning
 lettuce (optional)
 1 tomato, sliced (optional)

Peel, devein, and rinse shrimp. Fill a one-quart pot with hot tap water and bring to a boil. Place shrimp in water and cook for 2 minutes. Remove shrimp and chill under cold running water. Cut shrimp in half or leave whole for a more elegant salad. Mix shrimp, celery, and mayonnaise in a bowl. Sprinkle with lemon-pepper seasoning, and Old Bay or seafood seasoning.

Serving options: Serve on pita bread, toasted whole wheat or white bread, or hard rolls with shredded lettuce and fresh sliced tomato. Can also be served over lettuce as a salad.

SERVES: 4

SIDE DISH SUGGESTIONS: Potato chips and sweet pickles.

SHARK SALAD

 1 pound shark steaks
 1 tablespoon butter
 1 teaspoon lemon-pepper seasoning
 1 head iceberg lettuce
 1 cucumber
 1 15¼-ounce can beets
 1 15-ounce can baby corn
 1½ cups French dressing
 2 tablespoons salted sunflower seeds

Pre-heat the broiler. Melt butter in the microwave, drizzle over shark and sprinkle with lemon-pepper seasoning. Broil shark for 10 minutes. Remove from oven and cool.

Chop lettuce and place in a large mixing bowl. Peel cucumber and slice into ¼-inch slices. Add cucumber, drained beets, and baby corn to mixing bowl. Cut shark into ¼-inch cubes and add to salad. Pour dressing over salad and toss. Sprinkle with sunflower seeds and serve.

SERVES 4 to 6.

SIDE DISH SUGGESTIONS: Iced tea and flavored crackers.

PACIFIC RIM SHARK SALAD

1 pound shark steak
2 tablespoons olive oil
1 clove garlic, chopped
½ teaspoon grated ginger root
1 can bean sprouts
1 cup fresh or frozen snow peas
3 tablespoons vinegar
¼ cup olive oil
½ cup sherry
¼ teaspoon brown sugar
1 teaspoon soy sauce
1 can water chestnuts
1 head of leafy lettuce
1 can mandarin orange slices

Cut shark into small cubes and sauté in saucepan with 2 tablespoons oil, garlic, ginger, bean sprouts, and snow peas. Cook on low heat until shark turns white and snow peas are crisp and bright in color. Remove from heat and allow shark sauté to cool in refrigerator for one hour.
Dressing: Mix vinegar, ¼-cup oil, sherry, sugar, and soy sauce. Combine cold shark sauté, water chestnuts, and lettuce in a large mixing bowl. Pour dressing over salad and garnish with mandarin orange slices.

SERVE 4 to 6.

SERVE WITH any Asian entree.

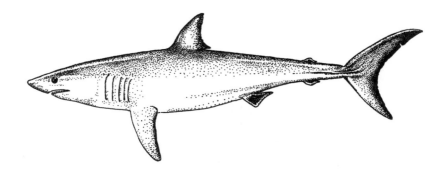

CALAMARI (SQUID) SALAD

    1 pound squid rings or 2 pounds cleaned whole squid
    3 stalks celery, chopped
    ½ bunch fresh parsley, chopped
    1 medium onion, chopped
    ½ cup cucumber, peeled and chopped
    ¼ cup olive oil
    3 tablespoons lemon juice
    ¼ cup vinegar
    ¼ teaspoon salt
    ¼ teaspoon pepper

Fill a 2-quart saucepan ¾ full of water and bring to a boil on high heat. Drop squid rings in water. If using whole squid, chop tentacles (discard head), and slice tubes into thin rings. Drop squid into water and boil until meat turns white. Remove from water, drain, and set aside. Mix chopped vegetables together in a large mixing bowl with squid, olive oil, lemon, vinegar, salt, and pepper. Chill in refrigerator for 2 hours. Serve cold.

SERVES 4 to 6.

SIDE DISH SUGGESTIONS: Crusty bread or pasta.

BELGIAN MUSSEL SALAD

    2 pounds live mussels
    1 red bell pepper, finely chopped
    1 green bell pepper, finely chopped
    1 cucumber, peeled and finely chopped
    2 sweet onions, finely chopped
    ¼ cup chopped black olives
    1 tablespoon fresh dill, chopped
    1 tablespoon lemon juice
    1 cup olive oil
    ¼ cup vinegar

Fill a large soup pot ¾ full of water. Place on high heat and bring to a boil. Rinse mussels in cold running water. Check mussels to be sure all are alive. Discard any mussels that do not close tightly after being disturbed by running water. Place mussels in boiling water and cook for 7 minutes. Drain mussels and pull meat from shells using a fork. Rinse mussel meat under cold running water and then set aside. In a large mixing bowl combine chopped peppers, cucumber, onions, black olives, and dill.

Mix gently and then add mussels, lemon juice, olive oil, and vinegar. Toss until all ingredients have been well blended. Place salad in refrigerator for 2 hours. Serve cold.

SERVES 4 to 6.

IMITATION CRABMEAT

In the early 1980s a new seafood item came into the market called *surimi*. It was a Japanese processed product consisting primarily of minced, white-fleshed fish (usually Alaskan pollack). The meat is pressed into large blocks and then frozen. The blocks are cooked, and other ingredients such as crab or crab extract, starch, red coloring, stabilizers, and spices are added. The product is rolled and cut into chunks or logs to simulate crab legs. The result is a semi-soft seafood product with a crab-like taste and texture. Surimi can also be used to imitate scallop, shrimp, or lobster meat and is sold fresh or frozen. Imitation crab is very low in calories and total fat per serving. Since surimi is fully cooked, it can be easily used in hot or cold dishes.

When purchasing surimi, take a minute to read the ingredient label. There are many brands on the market today. Some contain a portion of real crabmeat, while others use flavors and extracts. You will find some of the most common added ingredients to be: MSG, phosphates, sugar, salt, and sodium tripolyphosphate (STP). One or several of these additives may be restricted in your individual diet. Manufacturers are aware of these dietary needs and you will find certain surimi brands to be clearly labeled "NO MSG" or "NATURAL."

BASIC IMITATION CRAB SALAD

1 pound imitation crabmeat
½ cup mayonnaise
2 stalks celery, finely chopped
1 teaspoon lemon-pepper seasoning

Use imitation crabmeat as is for a chunky salad, or chop to the size that suits you best. In a large mixing bowl, mix meat, celery, mayonnaise, and lemon-pepper seasoning.

SERVES 4 to 6.

SERVING SUGGESTIONS: Place several tablespoons of salad on a bed of lettuce. Or serve on a fresh baked roll.

ZESTY SEAFOOD SALAD AND PARTY DIP

1½ pounds imitation crabmeat
2 yellow bell peppers
2 red bell peppers
1 medium red onion
2 bunches fresh parsley
1 cup mayonnaise
½ teaspoon lemon juice

Rinse peppers and parsley. Split peppers and remove seeds. Chop peppers, onion, and crabmeat into fine pieces. Finely chop parsley leaves. Add all chopped ingredients to a large mixing bowl. Combine with mayonnaise and lemon juice. This dish needs some time for all of the flavors to mix. Refrigerate for several hours or overnight.

SERVES 6 to 8.

SERVING SUGGESTION: Use as a dip. Serve with salt-free or fancy crackers.

CRABBY CHEF'S MASTER SALAD

1 pound imitation crabmeat
2 stalks celery
1 head iceberg lettuce
2 carrots
1 cucumber
2 heads romaine lettuce
1 cup baby ears of corn
1 cup flavored croutons
½ cup whole pitted black olives
½ cup whole green olives with pimento
½ cup shredded mozzarella cheese
favorite salad dressing

Chop celery and iceberg lettuce into coarse pieces. Peel carrots and cucumber. Slice cucumber into ¼-inch circles. Slice carrots julienne style. In a large salad bowl, mix iceberg lettuce, romaine lettuce, carrots, cucumber, celery, baby corn, and croutons. Place a serving of salad on salad plates and garnish tops of each with crabmeat, olives and mozzarella cheese. Add salad dressing of your choice.

SERVES 6 to 8.

PASTA PRIMAVERA WITH IMITATION CRABMEAT

1 pound imitation crabmeat
8 ounces rotini (twist pasta)
1 medium zucchini
2 carrots, peeled
½ cup scallions
1 small stalk broccoli
½ cup frozen peas
3 tablespoons olive oil
3 tablespoons grated Parmesan cheese
½ teaspoon chopped basil
½ teaspoon chopped thyme
½ teaspoon salt
½ teaspoon coarse black pepper
8 ounces half-and-half

Cook pasta according to package directions and drain. Chop zucchini, peeled carrots, scallions, and broccoli florets into bite-sized cubes. Heat the oil in a medium-sized skillet at medium/high heat. Sauté vegetables until they turn a bright color and are still crisp. Add imitation crab, cheese, basil, thyme, salt, pepper, and half-and-half to the vegetables. Bring to a boil and remove from heat. Mix with drained pasta in a large bowl and toss gently. Serve hot or cold.

SERVES 4 to 6.

SIDE DISH SUGGESTIONS: Warm bread sticks and honey butter, or pesto sauce.

See also:

King Neptune's Salad, page 161
Little Betsy's Crab, Shrimp, and Pasta Salad, page 162

SEAFOOD COMBINATIONS

CAPTAIN'S PLATTER WITH WHITE SAUCE

    1 pound scallops
    1 pound shrimp (any size)
    ½ pound white-fleshed fish fillets
    2 tablespoons butter
    2 tablespoons flour
    3 tablespoons dry white wine
    ¾ cup cream
    1 teaspoon grated Parmesan cheese
    ½ teaspoon salt
    ½ teaspoon pepper
    ½ cup buttery crackers, crushed

Pre-heat the oven to 325 degrees F. Peel and devein shrimp. In a
saucepan, melt butter and stir in flour. Cook on low heat until bubbly.
Add wine and cream, stirring constantly. When sauce has thickened,
add Parmesan cheese, salt, and pepper. Cut fish into chunks. Place
scallops, shrimp, and fish fillets in a baking dish. Pour wine sauce over
fish. Sprinkle crushed crackers over dish and bake for 5 minutes.
Switch the oven to broil and toast cracker topping until brown.

SERVES 4 to 6.

SIDE DISH SUGGESTIONS: String beans and scalloped potatoes.

LEMON-BUTTER SEAFOOD NUGGETS

1 pound monkfish or ocean catfish fillets
½ pound cooked crawfish tails or lobster meat
¼ cup butter
2 tablespoons lemon juice
1 teaspoon onion, minced
2 dashes Tabasco sauce
vegetable spray

Melt butter in a large saucepan; add minced onion and sauté until onion begins to soften. Add lemon juice and Tabasco sauce, and stir. Cut fish fillets into nugget-sized pieces. Place fish and crawfish or lobster meat in pan and sauté for 3 to 5 minutes. Remove from heat and serve hot.
SERVES 2 to 4.
SIDE DISH SUGGESTIONS: Peas and garlicky mashed potatoes.

SEAFOOD GUMBO

1 pound raw salad shrimp, peeled and deveined
8 ounces any cooked crabmeat
1 clove garlic, finely chopped
1 bunch scallions, finely chopped
1 red or green bell pepper, finely chopped
½ cup white rice
1 tablespoon olive oil
14 ounces okra, sliced
3 cups water
¼ teaspoon salt
¼ teaspoon Tabasco sauce
1 16-ounce can chopped tomatoes
¼ cup parsley, chopped
2 tablespoons cornstarch

In a deep skillet sauté for 5 minutes shrimp, garlic, scallions, sweet pepper, rice, olive oil, and okra. Add water, salt, Tabasco sauce, and tomatoes. Cover and simmer on low heat for 10 minutes. Mix cornstarch with ¼ cup water, pour into gumbo, stir until thickened, and let stand at low heat for 2 minutes. Remove gumbo from heat, ladle into serving bowls, and garnish with cooked crabmeat and parsley.
SERVES 4 to 6.
SIDE DISH SUGGESTION: Hot corn bread.

SEAFOOD JAMBALAYA

    8 ounces shrimp, peeled and deveined
    8 ounces scallops
    8 ounces crawfish meat
    2 strips bacon
    3 scallions
    1 green bell pepper
    3 stalks of celery
    ¼ cup chopped ham
    8 ounces smoked sausage
    ¼ cup parsley, chopped
    ¼ cup oil
    2 cups long-grain and wild rice
    1 14-ounce can chicken broth
    1 14-ounce can chopped peeled tomatoes
    ¼ teaspoon salt
    ¼ teaspoon cayenne pepper

Cut bacon, scallions, green pepper, celery, scallops, shrimp, ham, sausage, and crawfish meat into coarse pieces. Add parsley and stir-fry in a deep skillet with oil at medium heat for 3 minutes. Add rice and stir constantly for 2 minutes. Pour in chicken broth and tomatoes, and sprinkle with salt and cayenne pepper. Reduce heat to low, cover skillet, and cook for 20 minutes or until rice is soft.

SERVES 4 to 6.

SIDE DISH SUGGESTIONS: Crusty bread and chef's salad.

GODFATHER'S SEAFOOD DELIGHT

    1 pound shell-on shrimp, 16/20 count or larger
    12 littleneck clams
    1 pound mussels
    2 medium lobster tails
    1 pound angel hair pasta
    1 quart your favorite homemade or other pasta sauce
    2 tablespoons grated Parmesan cheese

Peel and devein shrimp. Cook pasta according to instructions on the package. Rinse clams and mussels to remove any sand. In a large saucepan, combine sauce, shrimp, clams, mussels, and split lobster tails, and bring to a bubbling simmer at medium heat. Reduce heat to low, cover pot, and simmer for 5 minutes, stirring once or twice each minute.

When pasta is cooked, remove from water and rinse under cold running water. Drain and arrange on serving dishes. Ladle sauce over each portion, making sure to spoon equal amounts of seafood onto each dish. Garnish with grated cheese.

SERVES 4.

SIDE DISH SUGGESTIONS: Tossed garden salad and garlic bread.

EASY CAPTAIN'S CATCH BOUILLABAISSE

10 shrimp (any size)
10 mussels
10 littleneck clams
10 bay or calico scallops (or 5 sea scallops cut in half)
1 lobster tail, 8 ounces or larger
1 pound white-flesh fish fillets
1 14½-ounce diced tomatoes
1 small can tomato paste
1 14½-ounce can chicken broth
2 cups water
2 tablespoons olive oil
1 teaspoon garlic, crushed or minced
¼ teaspoon saffron
1 bay leaf
½ teaspoon salt
½ teaspoon pepper
3 scallions, chopped
2 stalks celery, chopped

In a large soup pot, combine diced tomatoes, tomato paste, chicken broth, water, oil, garlic, saffron, bay leaf, salt, and pepper, and bring to a boil at high heat.

Peel and devein the shrimp. Remove meat from lobster tail. Cut lobster and raw fish fillets into small chunks. Add chopped scallions and celery and all of the seafood to the soup pot. Reduce heat to medium/high, and cook for 5 minutes. Reduce heat to low and simmer for 10 minutes. Remove bay leaf. Serve hot.

SERVES 6 to 8.

SIDE DISH SUGGESTIONS: Oyster crackers and tossed salad.

SEVEN STARS AROUND A FULL MOON

2 lobster tails
½ pound shell-on shrimp, 16/20 count or larger
½ pound bay scallops
½ pound boneless chicken breasts
½ pound imitation crabmeat
½ pound boneless pork loin
½ pound beef steak
2 cups white rice
½ cup cooking oil
1 can water chestnuts
1 6-ounce package frozen snow peas
1 can baby whole corn
½ cup oyster sauce
½ cup water

Cook rice according to instructions on the box. Remove lobster meat from tails and cut into chunks. Slice chicken, pork, and beef into thin slices. Peel and devein shrimp. Pre-heat the oil in large skillet at medium/high heat. Stir-fry all seafood and meat until cooked. Add water chestnuts, snow peas, corn, oyster sauce, and water. Stir vegetables, meat, and seafood for 2 minutes to mix in sauce.

Place cooked rice in a bowl. Pack it down tight, and then invert onto a large serving plate to form a moon-shaped mound. Arrange stir-fry medley around the moon and serve.

SERVES 4 to 6.

EAST-WEST MEDLEY

1 pound scallops (any type, fresh or frozen)
1 pound any white-fleshed fish fillets
1 red bell pepper
1 package bow-tie egg noodles
4 strips bacon
1 6-ounce package frozen snow peas
1 teaspoon garlic, crushed or minced
½ cup butter
1 teaspoon salt
1 teaspoon pepper
vegetable spray

Cut fish fillets and bell pepper into thin strips ½ inch long. Cook noodles according to instructions on the box. Microwave bacon until crisp and set aside. In a large non-stick skillet sprayed with vegetable spray, stir-fry fish, bell pepper, snow peas, and garlic at medium heat until fish is white. Add butter to skillet to melt. Remove from heat and mix with drained egg noodles. Sprinkle with salt and pepper and serve hot.

SERVES 4 to 6.

SIDE DISH SUGGESTIONS: Heated crusty bread and fresh tomato slices.

CIOPPINO BY THE BAY

½ pound cuttlefish or squid
1 pound shrimp (any size)
1 pound bay scallops
½ pound white-fleshed fish fillets
1 dozen littleneck clams or mussels
¼ cup olive oil
1 tablespoon garlic, crushed or minced
1 medium onion
1 green bell pepper
½ bunch fresh parsley
¼ teaspoon thyme
⅛ teaspoon saffron
salt and pepper to taste
1 28-ounce can peeled whole tomatoes
1 8-ounce can tomato sauce
¼ cup white cooking wine

Heat oil and garlic in a Dutch oven at medium/high heat. Peel and devein shrimp. Shuck the clams or mussels. Chop onion, green pepper, parsley, fish fillets, shellfish, and cuttlefish meats in coarse pieces. Sauté vegetables and all seafood until vegetables are soft. Reduce heat to medium; sprinkle with thyme, saffron, salt, and pepper. Add whole tomatoes, tomato sauce, wine, and cook for 10 minutes. Reduce heat to low, cover pot, and simmer for 30 minutes.

SERVES 4 to 6.

SIDE DISH SUGGESTIONS: Steamed rice and fresh fruit.

PAELLA

10 shrimp, 41/50 count or larger
2 lobster tails
6 littleneck or cherrystone clams
10 mussels
2 6-ounce boxes long grain and wild rice
1 pinch of saffron
1 cup sweet peas, fresh or frozen
¼ cup olive oil
1 cup water
1 cup cooking sherry
½ cup tomato sauce
1 bunch scallions, chopped
½ teaspoon garlic, crushed or minced
1 red or yellow bell pepper, chopped
½ pound boneless chicken breast
½ pound boneless pork loin
½ pound smoked sausage
1 teaspoon salt
1 teaspoon pepper
1 fresh tomato, diced

Prepare rice according to instructions on box, adding pinch of saffron to water. Add peas to rice during last 1 minute of cooking time.

Place olive oil, water, sherry, tomato sauce, scallions, garlic, and bell pepper in large deep skillet, and bring to boil at medium heat. Cut lobster tails in half lengthwise. Peel and devein shrimp, but leave tails intact. Rinse mussels and clams to remove any sand. Cut chicken, pork, and sausage into cubes. Add seafood, meat, salt, and pepper to broth. Cover skillet, reduce heat to low and let simmer for 10 minutes. Remove shrimp, lobster, mussels and clams from broth and set aside. Mix rice, broth, and peas, and then mound in a large deep serving dish. Arrange seafood around rice mound to create a colorful, festive look. Garnish with diced tomato.

SERVES 8 to 10.

SIDE DISH SUGGESTIONS: Crusty bread and tossed salad.

SCALLOP-SHRIMP-MUSHROOM MEDLEY WITH COCONUT

½ pound sea or bay scallops
½ pound shrimp, 26/30 count or larger
½ pound large fresh mushrooms
3 eggs
¼ cup milk
1 cup flour
4 cups vegetable oil
4 cups shredded unsweetened coconut

Peel and devein shrimp leaving tails attached. Remove straps from scallops. Remove stems from mushrooms and wash. Beat eggs with milk, and gradually add flour. Heat oil in deep pot at medium heat. Dip scallops, shrimp, and mushrooms in batter, and then roll lightly in coconut. Place each food separately (scallops, then shrimp, then mushrooms) in hot oil and cook until golden. (Oil temperature should be 320 to 350 degrees F.) Remove each piece from oil and allow excess oil to drain onto paper towel.

SERVES 2 to 3.

SIDE DISH SUGGESTIONS: Horseradish sauce for mushrooms and hot cocktail sauce for dipping the seafood.

KING NEPTUNE'S SALAD

½ pound cooked salad shrimp
½ pound real or imitation crabmeat, flaked
1 3⅔-ounce can smoked mussels
1 11-ounce can mandarin oranges
½ pound fresh spinach
2 hard-boiled eggs, diced
1 cup raspberry vinaigrette dressing
1 cup crisp Chinese noodles

Rinse spinach under cold water.

Drain juice from oranges. In a large bowl, toss spinach, shrimp, crab, mussels, oranges, and eggs with vinaigrette dressing. Top salad with crisp noodles.

Serves 4 to 6.

SIDE DISH SUGGESTION: Cottage cheese.

LITTLE BETSY'S CRAB, SHRIMP, AND PASTA SALAD

½ pound cooked salad shrimp
1 pound snow crab clusters (or ½ pound any cooked crabmeat)
1 pound elbow macaroni
1 8½-ounce can early June or baby peas
1 small onion, finely chopped
1 10-ounce can cream of mushroom soup
¼ cup milk
1 head iceberg lettuce

For freshest taste, use snow crab clusters. Pick meat from snow crab legs, claws, and body. Thaw salad shrimp and rinse in cold water. Cook elbow macaroni according to instructions on the box. Drain macaroni and rinse under cold running water. Drain again and chill in refrigerator. Drain water from canned peas. In a large bowl mix macaroni, crab, shrimp, onion, peas, cream of mushroom soup, and milk. Rinse lettuce, and layer a large serving dish with leaves. Mound seafood salad over lettuce.
SERVES 4 to 6.
SIDE DISH SUGGESTIONS: Potato chips and fresh tomato slices.

FUN WITH SUSHI

WHAT IS SUSHI?

Sushi (pronounced *soo-shee*) is a combination of cold rice, vegetables, and pickled fish rolled in a seaweed wrap. (It is also made as a vegetarian delicacy without fish.) The most common question people ask about sushi is, "Is it raw fish?" For the most part, the fish used in sushi is cooked or pickled. The popular misconception comes from the fact that sushi is Japanese in origin, and the Japanese often do include raw seafood in sushi in the form of *sashimi*—thin slices of high-grade **raw** fish, octopus, shrimp, and other seafood.

While you can have great fun with the entire family making sushi at home, it is recommended that all the fish you include in your sushi be cooked or pickled. Serving raw fish of certain species may pose some health risks. (See **How to Pickle Salmon and Tuna** below, for instructions on home pickling for sushi making.) Fish suitable for eating raw, and deemed to be "sashimi" grade, may be best and more safe to enjoy when prepared by a qualified sushi chef.

HOMEMADE SUSHI

Making sushi in the home is fun and easy. There is virtually no limit to the ingredients you can put in your sushi. That is what makes homemade sushi so intriguing. So be creative and explore new flavors. Try combinations of fruit and vegetables. Cooked seafood of any type can be used.

Basic ingredients and equipment

There are a few basic ingredients you will need for the best results: seaweed wraps, wasabi mix (hot paste), pickled ginger slices, seasoned rice vinegar, and soy sauce. Optional tools are an electric rice steamer, a bamboo sushi roller, and a good sharp knife. Many kitchen stores at local malls have sushi kits available. Seaweed wraps can be found at supermarkets or Asian markets.

A word about freshness

Plan to serve your homemade sushi the day it is prepared. The seafood and vegetables used in your sushi may last under proper refrigeration for several days. However, after just one day the rice will become stiff and be less enjoyable. Sushi is best made fresh and served within a few hours. The rice needs to be slightly sticky when cooked. Check during cooking and if too dry, add a few tablespoons of water.

TRADITIONAL GIANT CALIFORNIA ROLL

¼ pound imitation crabmeat
1 cup white rice
2 tablespoons seasoned rice vinegar
1 teaspoon sugar
1 teaspoon salt
1 fresh cucumber
5 sheets all natural seaweed
¼ cup soy sauce

Steam rice according to instructions on package. Place cooked rice in a metal bowl and add vinegar mixed with sugar and salt. Peel cucumber and slice in half lengthwise. Use a spoon to scrape seeds away, rinse under cold water and slice into thin strips. Place a full sheet of seaweed, shiny-side down, on cutting board. With a tablespoon, spread a ¼-inch layer of rice over half of the seaweed. In the center of the rice layer, place several strips of cucumber and imitation crab in a straight line across the width of the seaweed. Carefully roll the seaweed until a solid tube of rice has been formed around the cucumber and fish in the center. Place sushi roll in about a one-foot length of plastic wrap or bamboo roller and roll the sushi with a slight pressure to make the roll tight. Unwrap the plastic. Wait 2 minutes for rice and seaweed to set, and then cut sushi into ½-inch pieces. Serve with soy sauce for dipping. SERVES 6 to 8.

PICKLED TUNA OR SALMON AND VEGGIE ROLL

¼ pound pickled tuna or salmon
1 cup white rice
2 tablespoons seasoned rice vinegar
1 teaspoon sugar
1 teaspoon salt
1 fresh cucumber
1 fresh carrot
3 sheets all natural seaweed
¼ cup soy sauce

Steam rice according to instructions on package. When rice is cooked, remove from heat, place in a metal bowl, and add vinegar mixed with sugar and salt. Set aside to cool. Peel cucumber and carrot. Slice cucumber in half lengthwise. Use a spoon to scrape seeds away, rinse under cold water, and slice into thin strips. Cut carrot into thin strips. Cut seaweed sheets in half and place a half sheet of seaweed, shiny-side down, on cutting board. With a tablespoon, spread a ¼-inch layer of rice over half of the seaweed. In the center of the rice layer, place several strips of vegetables and tuna or salmon in a straight line across the short width of the seaweed. Carefully roll the seaweed until a solid tube has been formed around the fish and seaweed. Place sushi roll in about a one-foot length of plastic wrap or bamboo roller and roll the sushi with a slight pressure to make the roll tight. Unwrap the plastic. Wait 2 minutes for rice and seaweed to set, and then cut sushi into ½-inch pieces. Serve with soy sauce.
SERVES 6 to 8.

HOW TO PICKLE TUNA OR SALMON

1 pound tuna or salmon fillets
1 cup seasoned rice vinegar
2 teaspoons garlic, crushed or minced
1 medium red onion, finely chopped
1 teaspoon capers
½ cup olive oil

Cut fish fillets into 3-inch portions. Combine fish, vinegar, garlic, onion, capers, and olive oil in a deep bowl. Place in refrigerator and stir several times during the evening. On the next day, remove fish from pickling juice and slice thin for sushi. You can also enjoy this fish sliced thin and served with ginger sauce as a cold appetizer.

This fish can also be wrapped in freezer wrap in separate pieces instead of being sliced. Then, when you are ready to make sushi, you can thaw a piece as needed and slice.

IMITATION CRAB ROLL

½ pound imitation crabmeat
1 cup white rice
2 tablespoons seasoned rice vinegar
1 teaspoon sugar
1 teaspoon salt
3 sheets all natural seaweed
¼ cup soy sauce
¼ cup pickled ginger slices

Steam rice according to instructions on package. Place cooked rice in a metal bowl and add vinegar mixed with sugar and salt. Cut seaweed sheets in half and place a half sheet of seaweed, shiny-side down, on cutting board. With a tablespoon, spread a ¼-inch layer of rice over half of the seaweed. In the center of the rice layer, place pieces of imitation crab in a straight line across the short width of the seaweed. Carefully roll the seaweed until a solid tube has been formed around imitation crabmeat. Place sushi roll in about a one-foot length of plastic wrap or bamboo roller and roll the sushi with a slight pressure to make the roll tight. Unwrap the plastic. Wait 2 minutes for rice and seaweed to set, and then cut sushi into ½-inch pieces. Serve with soy sauce and pickled ginger slices. SERVES 6 to 8.

SMOKED SALMON OR SMOKED EEL AND VEGGIE ROLL

¼ pound smoked salmon or eel
1 cup white rice
2 tablespoons seasoned rice vinegar
1 teaspoon sugar
1 teaspoon salt
1 fresh cucumber
1 fresh carrot
1 small summer squash
3 sheets all natural seaweed
¼ cup soy sauce

Steam rice according to instructions on package. Place cooked rice in a metal bowl and add vinegar mixed with sugar and salt. Peel cucumber, carrot, and squash. Slice cucumber and squash in half lengthwise. Use a spoon to scrape cucumber and squash seeds away, rinse under cold water, and slice into thin strips. Cut carrot into thin strips. Cut seaweed

sheets in half and place a half sheet of seaweed, shiny-side down, on cutting board. With a tablespoon, spread a layer of rice ¼ inch thick over half of the seaweed. In the center of the rice layer, place several strips of vegetables and salmon or eel in a straight line across the short width of the seaweed. Carefully roll the seaweed until a solid tube has been formed around vegetables and fish. Place sushi roll in about a one-foot length of plastic wrap or bamboo roller and roll the sushi with a slight pressure to make the roll tight. Unwrap the plastic. Wait 2 minutes for rice and seaweed to set, and then cut sushi into ½-inch pieces. Serve with soy sauce for dipping.
SERVES: 6 to 8.

SHRIMP AND VEGGIE ROLL

¼ pound cooked salad shrimp
1 cup white rice
2 tablespoons seasoned rice vinegar
1 teaspoon sugar
1 teaspoon salt
1 fresh cucumber
1 fresh carrot
3 sheets all natural seaweed
¼ cup soy sauce

Steam rice according to instructions on package. Place cooked rice in a metal bowl and add vinegar mixed with sugar and salt. Peel cucumber and carrot. Slice cucumber in half lengthwise and use a spoon to scrape seeds away. Rinse under cold water and then slice into thin strips. Slice carrot into thin strips. Cut seaweed sheets in half and place a half sheet of seaweed, shiny-side down, on cutting board. With a tablespoon, spread a ¼-inch layer of rice over half of the seaweed. In the center of the rice layer, place several strips of cucumber, carrot, and a few pieces of cooked shrimp in a straight line across the short width of the seaweed. Carefully roll the seaweed until a solid tube has been formed around vegetables and shrimp. Place sushi roll in about a one-foot length of plastic wrap or bamboo roller and roll the sushi with a slight pressure to make the roll tight. Unwrap the plastic. Wait 2 minutes for rice and seaweed to set, and then cut sushi into ½-inch pieces. Serve with soy sauce for dipping.
SERVES 6 to 8.

LOBSTER, SESAME, AND CUCUMBER ROLL

¼ pound cooked lobster meat
1 cup white rice
2 tablespoons seasoned rice vinegar
1 teaspoon sugar
1 teaspoon salt
1 fresh cucumber
3 sheets all natural seaweed
1 tablespoon sesame seeds
¼ cup soy sauce

Steam rice according to instructions on package. Place cooked rice in a metal bowl and add vinegar mixed with sugar and salt. Peel cucumber, slice in half lengthwise, and use a spoon to scrape seeds away. Rinse under cold water and then slice into thin strips. Cut seaweed sheets in half and place a half sheet of seaweed, shiny-side down, on cutting board. With a tablespoon, spread a ¼-inch layer of rice over half of the seaweed. In the center of the rice layer, place several strips of cucumber and a few pieces of cooked lobster meat in a straight line across the short width of the seaweed. Sprinkle with sesame seeds. Carefully roll the seaweed until a solid tube has been formed around lobster and cucumber. Place sushi roll in about a one-foot length of plastic wrap or bamboo roller and roll the sushi with a slight pressure to make the roll tight. Unwrap the plastic. Wait 2 minutes for rice and seaweed to set, and then cut sushi into ½-inch pieces. Serve with soy sauce for dipping. SERVES 6 to 8.

MANGO AND CRAB ROLL

¼ pound imitation crab
1 cup white rice
2 tablespoons seasoned rice vinegar
1 teaspoon sugar
1 teaspoon salt
1 large fresh mango
2 teaspoons mayonnaise
3 sheets all natural seaweed
¼ cup soy sauce

Steam rice according to instructions on package. Place cooked rice in a metal bowl and add vinegar mixed with sugar and salt. Cut seaweed sheets in half and place a half sheet of seaweed, shiny-side down, on cutting board. With a tablespoon, spread a ¼-inch layer of rice over half of the seaweed. Peel mango and cut into thin strips. Mince crab and mix with mayonnaise. In the center of the rice layer, place several strips of mango and crab in a straight line across the short width of the seaweed. Carefully roll the seaweed until a solid tube has been formed. Place sushi roll in about a one-foot length of plastic wrap or bamboo roller and roll the sushi with a slight pressure to make the roll tight. Unwrap the plastic. Wait 2 minutes for rice and seaweed to set, and then cut sushi into ½-inch pieces. Serve with soy sauce for dipping. SERVES: 6 to 8.

TROPICAL ROLL

1 pound lobster or imitation crab, minced
1 cup white rice
2 tablespoons seasoned rice vinegar
1 teaspoon sugar
1 teaspoon salt
1 fresh cucumber
1 avocado
1 fresh orange or lime
2 teaspoons mayonnaise
3 sheets all natural seaweed
¼ cup soy sauce

Steam rice according to instructions on package. Place cooked rice in a metal bowl and add vinegar mixed with sugar and salt. Peel cucumber, avocado, and fruit. Slice cucumber in half lengthwise. Use a spoon to scrape seeds away, rinse under cold water and then slice into thin strips. Cut avocado and fruit into thin strips. Mince lobster or crab and mix with mayonnaise. Cut seaweed sheets in half and place a half sheet of seaweed, shiny-side down, on cutting board. With a tablespoon, spread a ¼-inch thick layer of rice over half of the seaweed. In the center of the rice layer, place several strips of vegetables and a few pieces of citrus in a straight line across the short width of the seaweed. Add lobster or crab meat. Carefully roll the seaweed until a solid tube has been formed. Place sushi roll in about a one-foot length of plastic wrap or bamboo roller and roll the sushi with a slight pressure to make the roll tight. Unwrap the plastic. Wait 2 minutes for rice and seaweed to set, and then cut sushi into ½-inch pieces. Serve with soy sauce. SERVES: 6 to 8.

VEGGIE ROLL

1 cup white rice
2 tablespoons seasoned rice vinegar
1 teaspoon sugar
1 teaspoon salt
1 fresh carrot
1 fresh cucumber
1 small summer squash
1 avocado
3 sheets all natural seaweed
¼ cup soy sauce

Steam rice according to instructions on package. Place cooked rice in a metal bowl and add vinegar mixed with sugar and salt. Peel cucumber, carrot, avocado and squash. Slice cucumber and squash in half lengthwise. Use a spoon to scrape seeds away, rinse under cold water and then slice into thin strips. Cut carrot and avocado into thin strips. Cut seaweed sheets in half and place a half sheet of seaweed, shiny side down, on cutting board. With a tablespoon, spread a ¼-inch layer of rice over half of the seaweed. In the center of the rice layer, place several strips of vegetables in a straight line across the short width of the seaweed. Carefully roll the seaweed until a solid tube has been formed around vegetables. Place sushi roll in about a one-foot length of plastic wrap or bamboo roller and roll the sushi with a slight pressure to make the roll tight. Unwrap the plastic. Wait 2 minutes for rice and seaweed to set, and then cut sushi into ½-inch pieces. Serve with soy sauce for dipping.
SERVES: 6 to 8.

HOLIDAY AND PARTY
SEAFOOD SPECIALTIES

HOLIDAY DISHES AND PARTY TREATS

Certain holidays are naturally associated with traditional festive
seafood dishes. In Jewish cultures, dishes made from whitefish, carp,
and pike are the most favored during the Yom Kippur, Rosh Hashanah,
and Passover holidays, as well as being used to make homemade gefilte
fish. Christmas Eve is the single biggest day for seafood sales in North
America and in Europe, where Italian, Greek, Spanish, Portuguese, and
Scandinavian cultures enjoy a large selection of seafood dishes on this
day. Mother's Day and Valentine's Day are the two favorite holidays for
live lobster and lobster tails. Then of course there is the Lenten season,
beginning Ash Wednesday and ending on Easter Sunday, when
Catholics throughout the world reduce or eliminate the consumption
of meat on Fridays and enjoy eating more seafood.

The recipes in this chapter offer many traditional holiday specialty
favorites as well as party treats such as dips, cheese logs, appetizers,
and seafood platters. They will add fun, flare, and excitement to your
special holiday gatherings, as you celebrate special occasions with
family and friends.

SEAFOOD CHEESE BALL WITH SLICED ALMONDS

1 pound imitation crabmeat or real crabmeat
2 8-ounce packages soft or whipped cream cheese
1 tablespoon mayonnaise
¼ teaspoon garlic powder
2 tablespoons onion powder
1 teaspoon seafood seasoning
½ cup sliced almonds, toasted
1 teaspoon paprika

Chop ½ pound crabmeat into fine pieces. Mix chopped crabmeat, cream cheese, mayonnaise, garlic and onion powders, and seasoning. Using hands, form mixture into a large ball. Spread almonds over a plate and roll the ball in nuts until fully covered. Sprinkle with paprika. Wrap in plastic wrap and refrigerate. At party time, slice the ball in half. Place each half on a platter and surround each with imitation crab flakes.
SERVES 10 to 12.
SERVE WITH assorted crackers.

SMOKED SALMON CHEESE LOGS WITH HAZELNUTS

1 pound smoked salmon slices
2 8-ounce packages soft or whipped cream cheese
1 tablespoon mayonnaise
2 tablespoons onion powder
¼ teaspoon garlic powder
1 teaspoon seafood seasoning
½ cup chopped hazelnuts
2 lemons
2 limes

Shred ¾ pounds of smoked salmon. Mix shredded salmon, cream cheese, mayonnaise, onion and garlic powders, and seasoning. Using hands, form mixture into several 2-inch thick logs. Spread hazelnuts over a plate and roll logs in nuts until fully covered. Wrap in plastic wrap and refrigerate. At party time, unwrap logs and place a few slices of smoked salmon over each. Garnish with thin slices of lemons and limes.
SERVES 10 to 12.
SERVE WITH assorted crackers.

CLAM AND PIMENTO DIP

12 cherrystone clams or 1 pound raw chopped clams
1 8-ounce package soft or whipped cream cheese
¼ cup clam juice
1 teaspoon onion powder
½ teaspoon garlic powder
¼ cup pimentos

Live Clams: Rinse clams to remove sand. Boil live clams until shells open wide. Remove the clams from the pot and chill under cold running water. Use a fork to pull meat from the shells. **Chopped Clams:** Boil the chopped clams until the meat becomes firm. Remove clams from the pot.

Mix cream cheese, clam juice, and onion and garlic powder. Chop clam meat and pimentos into fine pieces. Gently stir into cream cheese and mix well.

SERVES 8 to 10

CRAB AND CHEESE PARTY DIP

1 pound imitation crabmeat
1 teaspoon lemon-pepper seasoning
1 teaspoon onion powder
1 8-ounce package soft or whipped cream cheese
8 ounces soft cheddar cheese, softened
¼ cup milk
1 large round pumpernickel, rye or sweet Hawaiian bread
assorted crackers

Chop imitation crabmeat into fine pieces. Sprinkle with lemon-pepper and onion powder; then mix crab with both cheeses and milk. Shave the top ½-inch off the bread. With fingers, pull the center out of the bread, leaving a ½-inch wall. Fill the bread with crab and cheese dip. Take the bread you pulled from the center of the loaf and cut it into 1-inch cubes. Place the party dip bread in the center of a holiday platter and arrange bread cubes around the edge of the platter with assorted crackers.

SERVES 10 to 12.

SIDE DISH SUGGESTIONS: Olives and celery sticks.

BIRD'S NEST CAJUN CRAB DIP

1 pound real or imitation crabmeat
2 tablespoons onion powder
1 teaspoon paprika
¼ teaspoon garlic powder
1 tablespoon Cajun seasoning
2 8-ounce packages soft or whipped cream cheese
1 tablespoon mayonnaise
¼ teaspoon Tabasco sauce
1 large red cabbage
1 package alfalfa sprouts
assorted crackers

If using real crabmeat, pick through and remove all shells. If using imitation crabmeat, chop flakes into fine pieces. Sprinkle with onion, paprika, garlic powder, and Cajun seasoning. Mix mayonnaise, cream cheese, and Tabasco. Combine with crabmeat and turn gently with a spoon.

Cut cabbage in half. Use a knife to cut out the center leaving shells an inch thick. Fill both halves of the shelled cabbage with Cajun crab dip.

Place alfalfa sprouts on a large holiday serving platter. Center cabbage halves on plate to create a bird's nest effect. Circle outer edges of the plate with assorted crackers.
SERVES 10 to 12.

SMOKED SALMON PARTY DIP

4 to 6 ounces smoked salmon fillets
16 ounces soft or whipped cream cheese
Choices for added flavor:
¼ cup chopped chives, ¼ cup crushed peppercorns, ¼ cup
chopped dill, or any favorite seasoning or herbs

Using fingers or a knife, break up smoked salmon into small bits in a large mixing bowl. Sprinkle with your choice of seasoning and gently fold in cream cheese until mixture is consistent.

Presentation ideas

1. Place salmon party dip in a decorative bowl. Center the bowl on a large fancy dish and surround the bowl with a variety of crackers.
2. Purchase a large round rye, sour dough, or pumpernickel bread. Carve out the center; place the dip in cavity. Place bread on a large decorative plate and surround with a variety of crackers.

SERVES 5 to 7.

BLACK TIE AFFAIR LOBSTER-CAVIAR DIP

2 6-ounce lobster tails
2 or more ounces black caviar (from whitefish or lumpfish)
2 tablespoons sour cream
2 8-ounce packages soft or whipped cream cheese
3 tablespoons milk
1 teaspoon salt
½ teaspoon pepper
½ teaspoon onion powder
½ teaspoon garlic powder
1 teaspoon seafood seasoning
6 drops red food coloring
1 teaspoon paprika
2 black peppercorns

Fill a saucepan ¾ full with hot tap water. Place on high heat and when water reaches a hard boil, add lobster tails. Cook until shells turn red (about 3 minutes). Remove lobster tails and chill in cold water.

In a medium-sized mixing bowl combine sour cream, cream cheese, milk, salt, pepper, onion and garlic powders, seafood seasoning, and red food coloring. Blend until creamy. Split lobster tails using a scissors, but do not split the tail fin. Remove the meat with a fork. Cut the tail off of shell at last segment. Chop the lobster meat into fine pieces. Using a fork, mix the meat into the dip mix.

Turn finished dip out in a loaf shape onto a decorative serving dish. Carefully smooth edges to round them. Fan one of the lobster tails open and stick it into one end of the dip. Cover with plastic wrap and refrigerate overnight.

Before serving, sprinkle dip with paprika and decorate with caviar, using it to create a black bow tie or outline sections of a lobster's body. Use 2 peppercorns for the eyes.

SERVES 8 to 10.

SERVE WITH assorted crackers and vegetable strips.

FRIED CRAB BALLS

1 pound real or imitation crabmeat
2 slices dry bread
1 teaspoon Old Bay Seasoning
1 teaspoon baking soda
1 egg
2 tablespoons mayonnaise
1 tablespoon Worcestershire sauce
1 teaspoon dry or wet mustard
2 cups flour
½ cup vegetable oil

Check real crabmeat for shells and place meat in large bowl. Crumble dry bread over crabmeat. Sprinkle Old Bay Seasoning and baking soda over meat. In a small bowl whisk egg, mayonnaise, Worcestershire sauce, and mustard. Pour egg mixture into crabmeat bowl and mix gently with hands. Shape into tight, round 1-inch balls. Spread flour on a large sheet of waxed paper, and roll each crab ball to cover thoroughly with flour. Pre-heat the oil in a skillet at medium/high heat. Fry crab balls until golden. Turn as needed. (The only raw ingredient in the recipe is the egg. Cooking time needs only be long enough to brown crab ball and heat inside). Place a small bowl of cocktail sauce in center of a holiday platter. Surround sauce with crab balls. Serve hot or cold. SERVES 6 to 8.

SPINACH AND GARLIC CRAB BALLS

½ pound imitation crabmeat
1 block frozen chopped spinach
2 slices dry bread
1 teaspoon baking soda
1 tablespoon Parmesan cheese
1 egg
2 tablespoons mayonnaise
2 teaspoons garlic, crushed or minced
1 tablespoon onion, minced
vegetable spray
2 red bell peppers

Pre-heat the oven to 425 degrees F. Thaw spinach and mix with crabmeat in large bowl. Crumble dry bread over crabmeat. Sprinkle baking soda and Parmesan cheese over crab/spinach mixture. In a small bowl whisk egg, mayonnaise, garlic, and onion. Pour liquid into crabmeat bowl, and then mix gently with hands. Shape into tight, round 1-inch balls. Spray a baking tray with vegetable spray. Place crab/spinach balls on pan and bake for 15 minutes.

Slice red pepper into thin slices. Arrange pepper slices around a party platter and mound crab/spinach balls over pepper slices. SERVES 6 to 8.

PLANNING SHRIMP PARTY PLATTERS

Elegant party platters are easy to prepare in the home. Select shrimp that is 36/45 count or larger. Keep in mind that once cooked and deveined, your finished shrimp will be 25 to 50 percent smaller than when raw. When determining how much you will need to make a platter, the rule of thumb is ¼ pound of raw edible meat per person. For easy calculation, plan to have 10 to 12 shrimp per person.

SHRIMP AND IMITATION CRABMEAT PLATTER

2 pounds shell-on shrimp, 36/45 count or larger
1 pound imitation crabmeat flakes or legs

Cocktail sauce:
1 cup ketchup
1 tablespoon horseradish
1 dash hot sauce

Garlic sauce:
½ cup margarine
½ teaspoon garlic, crushed or minced

2 lemons
1 bunch fresh kale

Peel, devein, and rinse shrimp, leaving tails on. Fill a large soup pot ¾ full of hot tap water. Bring water to a boil. Add shrimp to boiling water and cook for three minutes. Remove a shrimp to check center for proper doneness.

Select a 12-inch holiday platter or serving dish. Mix cocktail sauce in a small bowl. Melt margarine and mix with garlic in a small bowl. Place both dipping bowls in the center of the platter.

Rinse kale and layer it around platter. Begin placing shrimp around one-half of the platter and crabmeat around the other. If using imitation crab legs, slice them on a diagonal in three pieces. Slice lemons thin, cut each slice ¾ of the way through slice and then twist the slice. Garnish the platter with the twisted lemons. Cover the tray with plastic wrap and refrigerate until party time. Serve with fancy toothpicks. SERVES 10 to 12.

SHRIMP PARTY PLATTER

5 pounds shell-on shrimp, 36/40 count or larger
2 bunches fresh kale
2 lemons

Cocktail sauce:
2 cups ketchup
2 tablespoons horseradish
½ teaspoon hot sauce

Peel, devein, and rinse shrimp, leaving tails on. Fill a large soup pot
¾ full of hot tap water. Bring water to a boil. Add shrimp to boiling water
and cook for three minutes. Remove a shrimp and check center for doneness. If cooked to your satisfaction, remove shrimp from water, and
immediately chill down by rinsing shrimp under cold running water, then
burying it in a bowl of ice. Cold water and ice stops the internal cooking
process and gives the shrimp a nice snappy cocktail crunch when eaten.

Select a 12- to 16-inch holiday platter. Mix cocktail sauce in a
decorative bowl and place in center of the platter. Rinse kale and layer
it around platter. Place shrimp around platter, building layer upon layer.

Slice lemons thin; cut each slice ¾ of the way through and then twist
the slice. Garnish the platter with the twisted lemons. Cover the tray with
plastic wrap and refrigerate until party time. Serve with fancy toothpicks.
SERVES 18 to 22.

SMOKED SEAFOOD WITH VARIETY CHEESE PARTY PLATTER

1 3⅝-ounce can each of
    smoked baby clams
    smoked oysters
    smoked mussels
4 ounces smoked salmon fillet, plain or other flavors
3 ounces sliced lox
8 ounces soft or whipped cream cheese
1 pound variety cheeses (3 types)
2 ounces any black caviar
2 ounces any red caviar
1 navel orange
1 box mini-crackers, any type

Drain the canned smoked seafood. Slice orange thinly. Place caviar in 2
small dishes, and place in center of platter. Circle caviar dishes with
orange slices.

Select a large serving tray. Shingle slices of oranges in center of tray. Roll each slice of lox with about 1 teaspoon of cream cheese. Around the orange slices, visually divide tray into 8 pie-slice sections and fill each section with one type of seafood or cheese.
SERVES 12 to 16.
SERVE WITH platter of fresh sliced vegetables.

FRIED FROG LEGS AND VEGETABLE PLATTER

This aquatic delicacy is most commonly found in the supermarket seafood section. Most frog legs are imported from China, where they are pond raised. Frog legs are very popular in the South, especially in Cajun country, where French cuisine is dominant. Restaurants usually buy small-sized legs, but supermarket shoppers find the larger legs most desirable.

  2 pounds frog legs
  1 cup vegetable oil
  2 eggs
  ¼ cup milk
  1 cup flour
  1 teaspoon Cajun seasoning
  ½ teaspoon salt
  1 cup ranch dressing
  1 teaspoon horseradish
  6 stalks celery
  3 carrots
  1 head of cauliflower

Pre-heat the oil in a skillet at medium/high heat. Beat eggs with milk in a bowl. Dip frog legs in egg wash.

Spread flour mixed with Cajun seasoning and salt on a large sheet of waxed paper. Dredge legs in flour, and dip back into the egg wash. Coat with flour once more and fry until golden. Remove frog legs from oil and place them on a paper towel to drain excess oil.

Select a colorful party platter. Fill a medium-sized bowl with ranch dressing mixed with horseradish. Center the bowl of dip on the platter. Slice celery and carrots into strips. Cut cauliflower into florets. Arrange vegetables and fried frog legs around platter.
SERVES 8 to 10.

HOLIDAY APPETIZERS AND DINNER ENTREES

The following is a selection of seafood dishes for sit-down holiday dinners. Some of the appetizers and main dishes are associated with elegant dining out, but are nevertheless easy (and less expensive) to create at home. Others have an ethnic flair that makes them essential for special holiday home gatherings.

GEFILTE FISH

> 1½ to 2 pounds whole yellow pike
> 1½ to 2 pounds lake white fish
> 3 onions
> 4 cups water
> 1 teaspoon salt
> 1 teaspoon black pepper
> 3 tablespoons matzoh meal
> 2 egg yolks
> 1 carrot

Purchasing note: Instruct fish market clerk to head and gut the fish. Then have the fish filleted and skinned. Tell the clerk you want all the heads, bones, and skin placed in one bag and the fillets in another.

Slice 2 onions into a pot with 3½ cups of water, salt and pepper; add the entire contents of the fish head bag. Simmer at low heat for 1 hour. Strain fish parts and onions from broth. Bring the clear broth to a rolling boil. Grind the fish fillets in a food processor. Mince the remaining onion. Mix fish, minced onion, matzoh meal, ½ cup of water, and egg yolks, and form into small balls. Drop the fish balls into the boiling broth. Skin the carrot, slice thin and add to broth. Cook for 45 minutes. Remove the pot from the stove. Pour all contents into several smaller bowls and allow them to cool for approximately 30 minutes. Then place contents of all bowls into a large storage container and refrigerate overnight. Serve the gefilte fish balls by themselves or with jellied fish broth.

SERVES 10 to 12.

SERVE as an appetizer.

STUFFED MUSHROOM CAPS

16 ounces crabmeat
2 tablespoons butter
¼ cup celery, chopped
¼ cup onion, chopped
1 slice of bread
2 eggs
4 tablespoons mayonnaise
¼ teaspoon mustard
¼ teaspoon seafood seasoning
24 large fresh mushrooms
vegetable spray

Pre-heat the broiler. Melt butter in a skillet, add celery and onion and
cook until soft. Crumble slice of bread. In a bowl, mix bread, eggs,
mayonnaise, mustard, seafood seasoning, crabmeat, celery, onion, and
crumbled bread. Remove stems from mushrooms and rinse caps under
cold running water. Dry caps with paper towel. Use a sharp knife to
slice a small piece off top of each mushroom so that they will stand
upside down flat on tray.

Make meatball-sized portions of crabmeat stuffing and firmly push
one into each mushroom. Spray the broiler tray with vegetable spray.
Place mushrooms on tray and broil 4 inches from heat until stuffing
begins to brown. Remove from oven and serve hot.

SERVES 8 to 10.

SERVE as appetizer with any dinner entrée.

HERRING IN CREAM SAUCE

12 medium-sized herring (pickled or smoked) fillets
1 cup sour cream
1 teaspoon fresh dill, finely chopped
½ teaspoon lemon juice
¼ cup yogurt
½ teaspoon vinegar

Cut herring fillets into three pieces. In a medium-sized mixing bowl,
combine sour cream, chopped dill, lemon juice, yogurt, and vinegar.
Gently turn herring fillets into the sauce. Refrigerate overnight to
allow flavors to mix.

SERVES 6 to 8.

SERVE as an appetizer before any dinner entrée.

HERRING IN WINE SAUCE

12 medium-sized herring (pickled or smoked) fillets
1 cup dry white wine
1 teaspoon dill
2 medium onions, thinly sliced
1 teaspoon lemon juice
½ cup vinegar
1 teaspoon mustard seeds
1 tablespoon sugar

Cut herring fillets into three pieces. In a medium-sized mixing bowl, combine wine, dill, onions, lemon juice, vinegar, mustard seeds, sugar, and herring. Stir and taste the sauce. If too tart, add more sugar to taste. If too sweet, add more vinegar.

SERVES 6 to 8.

SERVE as an appetizer before any dinner entrée.

ESCARGOTS IN GARLIC BUTTER

Escargots, or sea snails, can be found in most supermarkets, sold in cans with meat and shells separate. You will find them in the canned fish or imported foods aisle. This expensive restaurant appetizer can be prepared easily in the home for a fraction of the dining-out cost.

12 giant pre-cooked snails
12 snail shells
½ cup butter, softened
3 tablespoons garlic, crushed or minced
¼ teaspoon salt
¼ teaspoon black pepper

Pre-heat the oven to 400 degrees F. Combine butter, garlic, salt, and pepper in bowl. Insert one snail per shell and fill the remainder of the shell with garlic butter stuffing.

Select 2 small baking dishes and place 6 snails in each dish. Bake for 10 to 15 minutes. Serve escargots hot from the oven.

SERVES 6.

SERVE as an appetizer before any dinner entrée.

FRIED CALAMARI RINGS

1 pound cleaned squid (calamari) rings
2 cups vegetable oil
2 eggs
½ cup milk
1 teaspoon salt
½ teaspoon black pepper
1 cup flour
½ cup cornmeal

Rinse calamari under cold running water. Pre-heat the oil in a deep pot at medium/high. Mix eggs, milk, salt, and pepper in a bowl. Place rings in egg wash. Combine flour and cornmeal in a Ziploc bag. Drop squid rings into the bag, seal it, and shake to coat rings. Fry until golden. Drain on paper towel. Serve with cocktail sauce.

SERVES 4 to 6.

SERVE as an appetizer before any dinner entrée.

STUFFED CALAMARI

2 pounds large-tube (5- to 8-inch) cleaned squid (calamari)
2 pounds ricotta cheese
2 egg yolks
1 cup grated Parmesan cheese
¾ tablespoon dried parsley
1 tablespoon salt
1 tablespoon grated nutmeg
vegetable spray
1 small jar of your favorite pasta sauce

Pre-heat the oven to 425 degrees F. Fill a 2-quart saucepan ¾ full of hot tap water. Bring water to a boil. Rinse squid tubes under cold running water. Then blanch the squid for 3 minutes in the boiling water. Drain water and set aside the tubes to cool.

In a large bowl mix ricotta cheese, egg yolks, Parmesan cheese, parsley, salt, and nutmeg. Spray a large baking pan with vegetable spray. Fill each calamari with cheese stuffing and place in a single layer onto pan. Cover with sauce and bake stuffed squid for 30 minutes.

SERVES 4 to 6.

SIDE DISH SUGGESTIONS: Garlic bread and tossed salad.

GREEK SQUID SAUTÉ

2 pounds squid rings
2 tablespoons olive oil
½ bunch scallions, chopped
1 teaspoon garlic, crushed or minced
½ teaspoon salt
½ teaspoon pepper
¼ teaspoon oregano
2 cups tomatoes, chopped
¼ cup white wine
¼ cup Greek olives, pitted and chopped

Heat oil in a medium-sized skillet at medium heat. Sauté chopped
scallions and garlic until soft. Add squid rings, salt, pepper, and
oregano, and stir for 1 minute. Pour in tomatoes, wine, and olives.
Reduce heat to low, cover the skillet, and simmer for 30 minutes.
Check squid for tenderness. If more time is needed, cook 10 more
minutes and re-check squid.

SERVES 4 to 6.

SIDE DISH SUGGESTIONS: Greek salad and crusty bread.

OCTOPUS ("PULPO") PIE

1 pound octopus (cleaned, skinned, and diced)
2 large potatoes
3 carrots
1 small onion
1 cup frozen peas
1 quart heavy cream
1 teaspoon salt
1 teaspoon pepper
¼ cup water
3 tablespoons flour
2 9-inch pie shells

Peel and dice potatoes, carrots, and onion. Boil vegetables and octopus
until tender, about 20 minutes. Drain vegetables and pulpo and set
aside. Thaw one pie shell.

Pre-heat the oven to 325 degrees F. In a saucepan, heat cream at low
heat. When cream begins to bubble, add salt and pepper. Mix water with
flour and slowly add to cream, stirring until the sauce thickens.

Remove from heat, and add cooked vegetables, octopus, and peas. Pour mixture into frozen pie shell. Use thawed pie shell for top. Poke three holes to let steam escape. Bake pie for 15 minutes. Slice and serve.
SERVES 4 to 6.
SIDE DISH SUGGESTION: Broccoli.

FRESH EELS IN WINE SAUCE
  2 pounds fresh eels
  3 medium onions, chopped
  2 tablespoons flour
  2 tablespoons olive oil
  1 teaspoon salt
  1 teaspoon pepper
  1 tablespoon capers
  1 teaspoon lemon juice
  2 tomatoes, chopped
  1 cup red wine
  ¼ cup milk

Pre-heat oven to 325 degrees F. Sauté onion, flour, and oil in a saucepan on low heat. Add salt, pepper, capers, lemon, oil, tomatoes, and wine. Cook at low heat for 3 to 5 minutes. When sauce begins to bubble, mix flour with milk and stir into sauce until it thickens.

Cut eels into 3-inch pieces and place in a single layer in a baking dish. Pour sauce over eels and bake for 20 to 30 minutes.
SERVES 6 to 8.
SIDE DISH SUGGESTIONS: Boiled parsley potatoes, onion soup, and hot, freshly baked bread.

See also: **Zesty Seafood Salad and Party Dip,** page 152

GLOSSARY OF SEAFOOD TERMS

Aquaculture. A system of "farm-raising" seafood, in which growth, feed, environment, and harvest of the species are regulated through human intervention.

Cephalopods. A class of mollusks (including octopus, squid, and cuttlefish) with a tubular siphon under the head and muscular arms around the head.

Cross contamination. Contamination that occurs when the bacteria present in raw foods are transmitted to cooked foods (through handling, for example).

Crustaceans. A class of arthropods (including crab, lobster, shrimp, and crawfish) with external skeletons, jointed legs, and two pairs of antennae.

Dry pack. Seafood packed without treatment with sodium tripolyphosphate (STP).

Extensive aquaculture. A method requiring the least amount of human intervention and relying more on the natural environment.

Fillet. Fish sliced with (in the direction of) the bone rather than against it; fillet is usually comparatively free from bones.

H&G. Whole fish that has had the head and guts removed.

Intensive aquaculture. A method requiring full human intervention from start to finish.

IQF. "Individually quick frozen." Each piece of seafood is ice-glazed and can be removed from the package one at a time.

Mollusks. A large phylum of invertebrate animals enclosed in shells. Popular commercial species are uni-valve, two-shelled filter feeders: clams, mussels, oysters, and scallops.

MSG. Monosodium glutamate, a flavor enhancer.

Omega-3s. Polyunsaturated fatty acids found in fish and shellfish. Omega-3s relax the arteries and improve blood circulation, thus inhibiting the formation of blood clots.

Pathogenic bacteria or viruses. Two types of illness-causing micro-organisms that may be present on raw food or transmitted by food handlers. Examples are staphylococcus and *E. coli* bacteria and hepatitis viruses. Most are successfully killed with proper cooking.

Pin bone. Row of fine bones that may be found at the center of a fish fillet.

P&D. Referring to shrimp: "Peeled and deveined."

PUD. Referring to shrimp: "Peeled and undeveined."

Rigor mortis. The stiffening of tissue following death.

Sashimi. Very thin slices of high-grade **raw** fish, octopus, shrimp, or other seafood.

Semi-intensive aquaculture. A method requiring minimal human intervention.

Sodium tripolyphosphate (STP). An additive used to protect seafood from dehydration during the freezing process. Excessive amounts cause seafood to absorb excessive water.

Surimi. Imitation crabmeat produced from various types of fish (usually Pacific pollock) with a flavor similar to crab.

Sushi. (Pronounced *soo-shi)* A combination of cold rice, vegetables, and pickled fish rolled in a seaweed wrap.

Vibrio bacteria. Bacteria that produce marine toxins associated with molluscan shellfish. These toxins can occur both naturally and as a result of pollution. Certain Vibrio toxins can produce serious illness, especially in individuals with compromised immune systems.

Wet pack. Seafood that has been treated with sodium tripolyphosphate (STP).

TRADE ORGANIZATIONS AND GOVERNMENT AGENCIES

CDCP: Center of Disease Control and Prevention.

FAO: Food and Agriculture Organization of the United Nations.

FDA: Food and Drug Administration, the U.S. regulatory authority for seafood. FDA Seafood Hotline: 1-800-FDA-4010.

NFI: National Fisheries Institute, seafood trade organization that represents industry and provides information to the general public pertaining to seafood.

USDC: United States Department of Commerce, the branch of the U.S. government that regulates and promotes U.S. seafood commerce worldwide.

NMFS: National Marine Fishery Services, the branch of the USDC responsible for seafood inspection, grading, and standards for the seafood industry.

NOAA: National Oceanic Atmospheric Administration, a branch of the USDC that provides research and statistical studies of the ocean.

Note: Most states that harvest or process seafood have a bureau of seafood or seafood promotion council. For more information about seafood in your state, contact those agencies in your area. Many also have websites—search under the state of your choice and seafood.

INDEX